ONLINE PLATFORMS, PANDEMIC, AND BUSINESS RESILIENCE IN INDONESIA

A JOINT STUDY BY GOJEK AND THE ASIAN DEVELOPMENT BANK

2023

Contents

Tables and Figures

Foreword

Gojek

Gojek is Southeast Asia's leading mobile on-demand services and payments platform, founded on the principle of using technology to remove life's daily frictions by connecting consumers to the best providers of goods and services in the market. The company first focused on courier and motorcycle ride-hailing services before launching its app in January 2015 in Indonesia. Gojek has since expanded into Singapore, Thailand, and Viet Nam, providing access to a wide range of services from transportation and digital payments to food delivery, logistics, and many other on-demand services. In May 2021, Gojek and technology company Tokopedia combined their businesses to form GoTo Group, the largest technology group in Indonesia and the "go-to" ecosystem for daily life. GoTo brings together the strengths of two Indonesian champions and creates a globally unique and highly complementary ecosystem that combines e-commerce, on-demand, and financial services.

In 2020, Gojek partnered with the Asian Development Bank (ADB) to carry out a joint research project on the impact of the coronavirus disease (COVID-19) on the digitalization of Indonesian micro, small, and medium-sized enterprises (MSMEs). ADB and Gojek agreed to share certain confidential and proprietary information with one another to facilitate this joint study. To supplement the information collected from the study's survey of 869 MSME merchants active on our online platform, Gojek also made available for analysis weekly administrative and transactions data on nearly 300,000 GoFood merchants in Indonesia. Working in collaboration, Gojek and ADB were able to assess how COVID-19 affected the business operations of Indonesian MSMEs and the daily lives of merchants, while also identifying the benefits to MSMEs from their participation in the Gojek ecosystem.

We are pleased to present the outcome of this unique collaboration with ADB in this summary report and hope that it ultimately contributes to the improvement of our comprehensive service offerings for MSMEs in Indonesia.

Shinto Nugroho
Chief of Public Policy and Government Relations
Gojek

Asian Development Bank

The Asian Development Bank (ADB) invested over $20 billion in 2022 in sovereign and nonsovereign projects in developing member economies in Asia and the Pacific. Given the importance of micro, small, and medium-sized enterprises (MSMEs) in Asian economies—comprising more than 96% of all businesses and providing two out of three private sector jobs across the region—ADB views MSMEs' success as vital for the region's economic health.

In 2020, ADB and Gojek signed a memorandum of understanding to conduct a joint study on the impact of the coronavirus disease (COVID-19) on Indonesian MSMEs working through the GoFood platform, an on-demand food delivery service, and the benefits of digitalization for businesses using the Gojek ecosystem. This is ADB's first formal research collaboration with Gojek, one of Indonesia's prominent online platforms. This knowledge partnership provided valuable insights into the role platforms can play in generating employment opportunities and in bringing unbanked, underserved segments of the population closer to formal markets, integrating them into national value chains, and improving their resilience during the COVID-19 pandemic.

This report summarizes the findings from a national survey conducted among GoFood merchants. The survey provided insights into the impact of the pandemic on MSMEs and the entrepreneurs leading them, revealing differences in GoFood merchants' coping mechanisms across gender lines. They also unearth untapped opportunities that can potentially increase the impact of government support programs during crises such as the COVID-19 pandemic. We anticipate the findings of this research partnership will help shape policies that expand opportunities for unique and innovative online platforms like Gojek to further contribute to inclusive and sustainable development.

ADB extends its appreciation to Gojek for its full participation in this timely research collaboration that brought together one of Asia's leading online platforms and a development organization with a special focus on the region. We hope that the output of this partnership will be useful in strengthening the provision of services through Gojek's online platforms and improving the overall business environment in which MSMEs operate in Indonesia.

Albert Park
Chief Economist and Director General
Economic Research and Development Impact Department
Asian Development Bank

Abbreviations

ADB	Asian Development Bank
COVID-19	coronavirus disease
EJBN	East Java, Bali, and East and West Nusa Tenggara
GDP	gross domestic product
GMV	gross merchandise value
HS	high school
Jabodetabek	Jakarta, Bogor, Depok, Tangerang, and Bekasi
KUR	*Kredit Usaha Rakyat*
MSMEs	micro, small, and medium-sized enterprises
PEN	*Pemulihan Ekonomi Nasional*
PKH	*Program Keluarga Harapan*

Acknowledgments

The report was prepared by Gojek and the Asian Development Bank (ADB) teams led by Tricia Iskandar (Gojek) and Yesim Elhan-Kayalar (ADB), and it summarizes the key findings of the Gojek–ADB Joint Study. Gojek's Public Policy and Government Relations, Merchant Marketing, and Research Teams have made important contributions to the research project and report, which are hereby recognized with appreciation. The authors would like to thank Yasuyuki Sawada, Matthew Shum, and Yi (Daniel) Xu for their valuable insights during the study design phase, and to Gojek and ADB's Indonesia Resident Mission for their meticulous review of the report. The SMERU Research Institute supported the surveys. Jade Tolentino, Orlee Velarde, and Rhommell Rico provided copyediting and typesetting assistance.

Executive Summary

Micro, small, and medium-sized enterprises (MSMEs) provide jobs, generate income, and drive overall economic growth in Indonesia. In 2020, the MSME sector contributed approximately 61% to Indonesia's gross domestic product (GDP) and provided about 97% of total employment. The onset of the coronavirus disease (COVID-19) pandemic and subsequent restrictions on mobility threatened the viability of many Indonesian MSMEs, which experienced temporary shutdowns, cash shortages, and falling revenue.

MSMEs employed a variety of strategies to survive the pandemic, including shifting from physical to digital sales by marketing and selling their products through online platforms. The use of online platforms in regular business operations can strengthen MSMEs by (i) increasing the efficiency of sales and marketing operations; (ii) channeling new suppliers to business owners; (iii) offering financing options with low-interest rate loans; and (iv) providing business development training. Digitalization also requires technological adaptability and agility, or it risks leaving some behind, particularly merchants who are less educated and whose businesses are not located in metropolitan areas. This is why, even before the onset of the pandemic, MSMEs' digitalization was already on Indonesia's development agenda.

Gojek had an important role in the continued operation of MSMEs that otherwise would have been completely cut off from customers during strict pandemic lockdowns. Established in 2010 as a courier and ride-hailing service, by 2015, Gojek had expanded its service offerings to include an easy-to-use mobile application with a dashboard providing merchants with online marketing, sales, and payment support. By 2021, Gojek accounted for 43% of the $4.6 billion food delivery market in Indonesia. Its food delivery service application (app), GoFood, allows merchants to sell home-cooked food and have them delivered through the app's ride-hailing service.

Gojek and the Asian Development Bank (ADB) conducted a joint study to examine the COVID-19 pandemic's impact in Indonesia on MSMEs in the food and beverage sector that sell and market their products via the GoFood platform. The study's objective was to gain a better understanding of the digitalization process among Indonesian MSMEs and explore their resilience amid a long-lasting crisis such as the pandemic. The study comprised analyses of GoFood MSMEs' performance and experiences during the pandemic, with data generated from surveys among GoFood merchants and complemented with data from Gojek. The MSME survey comprised two stages—online and via phone—with Gojek implementing the online survey and the SMERU Research Institute conducting the phone survey with guidance from ADB and Gojek. Of the 869 GoFood merchants participating in the online survey, 375 agreed to be contacted for the phone survey, which itself had a participation rate of 73.3% (275 merchants). The report's findings rely primarily on the online survey data, which provide critical information on business size (as measured by number of employees) and the gender of the owner, allowing for comparisons to be made on the varying impacts of the pandemic on diverse groups. Data from online survey were supplemented with phone survey responses, as well as Gojek administrative data covering information such as merchants' registration, transactions, and routine operations.

Figure ES summarizes merchant responses when asked about Gojek's impact on their MSME during the pandemic. As can be seen, digitalization benefited the majority of MSMEs, including the most vulnerable. Most merchants (51.5%) stated that using GoFood helped their business survive the economic crisis, with an additional 41.8% crediting Gojek for helping expand their business in a particularly challenging economic environment.

Figure ES: Gojek's Impact on Micro, Small, and Medium-Sized Enterprises during the Pandemic

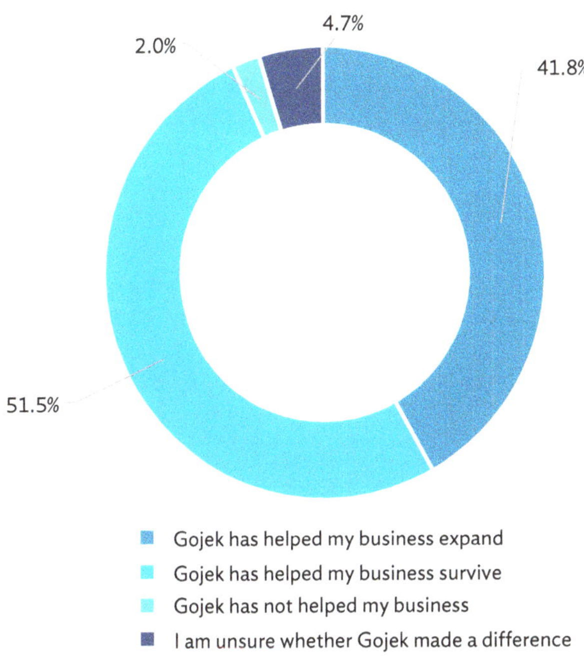

Note: The figures refer to Gojek's impact on businesses from March 2020 to February 2021.
Source: Online survey of GoFood merchants.

The survey's findings supported much of the literature on the adverse economic impacts of the COVID-19 pandemic, particularly for micro-sized and self-employed MSMEs. Those with low cash reserves were in the greatest peril of not surviving the pandemic. Meanwhile, Gojek continued to support businesses throughout the pandemic by offering business solutions that promote efficient operations (GoBiz), enable digital payments (GoPay), and offer financial services (GoModal). In facilitating the growth and resilience of MSMEs through its various digital business lines, Gojek has been investing in its own success.

While digitalization helped many vulnerable MSMEs endure the economic crisis, several daunting challenges had to be overcome. For example, women-owned MSMEs faced a "triple burden"—of business management, economic shock, and domestic responsibilities—which complicated their efforts to maintain a viable business amid a generational economic downturn. MSMEs in peri-urban and remote areas are often disadvantaged in delivering food to customers if additional delivery fees are required due to the distances involved in meal pickup and delivery. The nonavailability of delivery riders in these areas also hampered their online sales at times during the pandemic. These are challenges that lack easy solutions from online platforms alone and instead may require innovative, collaborative approaches by stakeholders from private and public sectors.

Amid many positives regarding platforms' support for MSMEs in Indonesia, there is scope for further development. For example, pandemic conditions led many MSMEs to either join for the first time or expand their presence on online platforms. While offering the opportunity to reach new customers, this also led to increased competition for many merchants who may have already been struggling to remain profitable even before the pandemic. Increased competition, in turn, adversely impacted the revenues and survival rate of businesses. A service area allocation algorithm that takes this aspect into account may help alleviate merchant overcrowding in specific service areas and contribute to enterprise sustainability.

While outside the scope of this study, it can be inferred from the survey findings that accessibility to a range of government assistance programs for MSME owners should be expanded. This can be accomplished through a combination of simplifying application processes and raising awareness through promotions that utilize a variety of media to reach different segments of the population. A regularly updated MSME database that is integrated across government institutions would help better identify beneficiaries and distribute needed assistance. While there may be administrative and technical hurdles to create such a database, its potential value to MSME merchants is evident in the survey responses of many participants. Many of them expressed their preference for—and yet unfamiliarity with—application procedures and other requirements for key government assistance programs. An opportunity exists to leverage the comparative advantage of online platforms that have real-time access to a wealth of transaction and financial data from hundreds of thousands of merchant–partners.

Gojek enabled MSMEs to enhance their visibility amid mobility restrictions and reach a wider customer base than otherwise would have been possible during the pandemic. For some, this meant survival in an extremely challenging economic environment. For others, Gojek helped facilitate the growth of their business by channeling new customers to them. The positive findings related to MSME resilience during the economic turmoil of the pandemic point to the benefits of digitalization in general. To facilitate an inclusive recovery and better equip MSMEs to deal with the next crisis, it is important to adequately prepare the MSME sector for a more digital future. The study's concluding observations offer insights for online platforms, policymakers, and other relevant stakeholders in supporting MSMEs and accelerating the process of recovery from the pandemic's most severe economic impacts.

I. Introduction

A. Overview of the MSME Sector in Indonesia and the Impact of the COVID-19 Pandemic

Micro, small, and medium-sized enterprises (MSMEs) are considered the pillar of Indonesia's economy, providing employment opportunities, generating domestic income, and helping to drive economic growth, all of which contribute to the reduction of poverty. In 2020, the MSME sector contributed approximately 61% to Indonesia's total gross domestic product (GDP) and accounted for more than 97% of total employment (Anatan and Nur 2003). Therefore, it was of great concern when the economic impacts of the coronavirus disease (COVID-19) pandemic threatened the sustainability of many Indonesian MSMEs. Government-imposed social distancing policies caused supply chain issues and difficulty in accessing raw materials, disrupted product distribution, and led to a decline in production activities (LPEM FEB Universitas Indonesia and UNDP 2020, Asiati et al. 2021). Compared to large businesses, MSMEs worldwide were hit harder by the pandemic due to their financial fragility and relative lack of resources (Bartik et al. 2020 and Eggers 2020). Specifically, MSMEs in Indonesia experienced temporary shutdowns, cash shortages, and falling revenue (Sonobe et al. 2021).

The Government of Indonesia supports MSMEs' development through a range of assistance programs, and these programs have been expanded during the pandemic. The government support programs for MSMEs and pandemic-related cash transfer programs include: (i) *Pemulihan Ekonomi Nasional* (PEN) or National Economic Recovery Program; (ii) *Kredit Usaha Rakyat* (KUR) or People's Business Credit program; (iii) Mekaar, a group-lending product for women who managed microbusinesses and earned less than $2 a day; (iv) Umi, a lending subsidy through nonbank financial institutions for microbusinesses; (v) Prakerja Card program, a pre-employment program for temporary social assistance and skills development; (vi) Sembako, a food voucher for poor households; and (vii) Program Keluarga Harapan (PKH), or Family Hope Program (Kementerian Ketenagakerjaan 2023). In addition, the Government of Indonesia responded to the negative economic impacts of the COVID-19 pandemic with a stimulus package worth about 6% of GDP that included tax relief, increased social assistance for low-income families, and incentives for MSMEs (Olivia et al. 2020). The expansion of social protection assistance was necessary since 81% of Indonesian households reported declining incomes (Morgan and Trinh 2021). As a further reflection of the pandemic's severe impacts, Indonesia was reclassified from upper-middle income to lower-middle income country status in the World Bank's classification of countries by income groups.

B. Contribution of Digitalization

MSMEs employed a variety of strategies to remain afloat during the pandemic. One such strategy was shifting from physical to digital sales by marketing and selling their products through online platforms. It is not surprising that the mobility restrictions implemented to slow the spread of the virus had a secondary effect of pushing more MSME sales online, accelerating the adoption of digitalization across the Indonesian economy.

One of digitalization's core benefits to MSMEs is reducing transaction costs by aggregating demand and supply through e-commerce platforms. Further, it allows firms to manage transactions easily through digital payment services, deliver products efficiently, and acquire new customers via online selling and marketing options. Several studies highlight that digitalization proved to be a lifeline for many businesses, including MSMEs, during the COVID-19 pandemic (Bank Indonesia 2022, UN Women 2020, Sonobe et al. 2021).

Digitalization also requires technological adaptability and agility, or it risks leaving some enterprises or individuals behind, particularly those who are less educated and whose businesses are not located in metropolitan areas. Hence, MSMEs' digitalization was a development priority in Indonesia even before the pandemic. Government efforts to help more MSMEs digitalize has included partnering with large enterprises to promote the adoption of digital tools for MSMEs, and collaboration with the Indonesian E-Commerce Association to help small businesses outside of Java become more digitally integrated through the provision of online classes (Eloksari 2020, Investment Coordinating Board 2021).

C. The Southeast Asian Food Delivery Landscape

The food delivery industry in Southeast Asia had a gross merchandise value (GMV) of $4.2 billion in 2019 on a year-on-year growth of 91%.[1] The COVID-19 pandemic would accelerate the industry's already impressive growth rate. Meal orders had surged across the board in response to mobility restrictions and as various stakeholders, including both online platforms and restaurants and other food providers, adapted to surging demand. In 2020, aggregate GMV in the food delivery sector reached $11.9 billion in the subregion, an increase of 183% year-on-year. While remaining robust the following year, annual growth eased to 30% in 2021, with Southeast Asia's food delivery GMV reaching $15.5 billion (Momentum Works 2021).

In terms of annual GMV, GoFood is one of the top three food delivery online platforms in Indonesia, along with Grab and Foodpanda. When it comes to being the consumer favorite, a significant majority (84%) of people who use more than one food delivery platform considers GoFood to be the best in Indonesia, according to research by Nielsen Singapore (2019). Specific characteristics that consumers appreciate are GoFood's diverse menu choices and merchants, user-friendly application, and speed of delivery (Kartono and Tjahjadi 2021). In terms of monthly order volume, leadership in the online food and grocery delivery industry is closely contested between market leaders Gojek and Grab. In the second half of 2021, both companies had similar market shares by order volume (Measurable AI 2023). During the second year of the pandemic, ordering convenient food became more deeply ingrained in consumers' lives, and online platforms sought to increase average transaction values by improving services and targeting different customer segments. In 2021, food and beverage merchants learned how to adjust to the online marketplace, increasing the share of their online sales. Some merchants capitalized on the expanded delivery infrastructure, expanded their menus, or introduced new brands.

In 2022, total food delivery GMV in Southeast Asia reached $16.3 billion (Momentum Works 2023). Even amid the more recent negative economic impacts of the pandemic—this time due to the spread of the omicron variant of COVID-19 and subsequent lockdown in the first half of the year—the Indonesian food delivery service market continued to expand (Google, Temasek, and Bain & Company 2022).

The reopening of economies over the course of the year, with increased in-person dining, had a major impact on the region's food delivery demand. In addition, rising interest rates triggered by monetary policy tightening in the United States created financing difficulties for tech firms, including major food delivery platforms. Third-party logistics firms—such as Lalamove, GrabExpress, and PandaGo—were also increasingly active in the food delivery market

---

[1]   The six Southeast Asian markets in descending order of 2020 gross merchandise value are Indonesia, Thailand, Singapore, the Philippines, Malaysia, and Viet Nam.

in Southeast Asia. Thus, competition intensified further for pure play (e.g., Foodpanda) and super app (e.g., Gojek, Grab) platforms in the food delivery ecosystem, making operational efficiency, as well as increased sales volume and density, key to maintaining growth.

D. Gojek and Its Business Solution, GoBiz

Since its establishment in 2010 as a call center offering instant courier and motorcycle ride-hailing services, Gojek has grown to become one of Indonesia's leading online platforms. By 2015, it had expanded its service offerings to include an easy-to-use mobile application providing merchants with online marketing, sales, and payment support. Specifically, the GoFood application in the Gojek ecosystem allows merchants to prepare home-cooked foods and have them delivered through the app's ride-hailing infrastructure.

At the core of the Gojek ecosystem is GoBiz, launched in 2019 as an all-in-one business solution, which today connects more than 500,000 merchant-partners with nearly 200 million Gojek app users in Indonesia.[2] GoBiz enables merchants to increase sales via an online delivery service that expands customers' reach and payment options for food delivery. GoBiz also helps merchants manage their business more efficiently and securely with a point-of-sale feature and consolidated transaction reporting. Merchants can regularly update their operating hours, prices, and menu on the GoFood app. Personal identification number validation between cashier and delivery rider facilitates smooth pick-up and delivery, while the point-of-sale feature records and monitors all online and dine-in transactions in a real-time integrated system. GoBiz' reporting features can be used to identify best-selling items, track favorite payment methods, and compare online versus dine-in sales. Finally,

promotions—such as menu discounts, vouchers, and free or reduced delivery fees for new or recurring customers—can be easily linked to social media apps.

In addition to GoBiz, Gojek has supported MSMEs by connecting GoFood merchants to suppliers (GoFresh), providing digital payment solutions (GoPay), and offering financial services such as zero-collateral working capital loans (GoModal) during the pandemic. By facilitating the success of MSMEs through increased sales, Gojek also expands its own revenue stream, creating a mutually beneficial scenario for merchants and the online platform.

In Indonesia, Gojek's primary Southeast Asian market, average order values rose from less than Rp40,000 in January 2019 to nearly Rp65,000 in December 2022, indicating the potential for continued gains in the post-pandemic era (Measurable AI 2023). In addition to market demand, profitability in the region's food delivery industry is also influenced by the topography and demographics of the delivery areas. Most of the urban population in Indonesia live and work in low-rise areas, not the more densely populated high-rise areas, which heavily influences lunch and dinner demand for GoFood services. Average basket (i.e., food order) sizes are small in Indonesian cities, while there is an abundance of low-wage riders on bicycles and motorcycles who can more easily navigate frequent traffic jams.

Amid the competitive Southeast Asian food delivery environment described above, Gojek held its strong position in the Indonesian market—comprising 43% and 44% of total GMV in 2021 and 2022, respectively. Gojek's merger in 2021 with Tokopedia, a consumer-to-consumer e-commerce platform, led to the creation of the GoTo Group, Indonesia's largest technology company. This partnership has provided additional opportunities to

---

2   The discussion on GoBiz is derived from: *Introducing GoBiz: Gojek as Business Growth Partner*. www.gobiz.co.id.

leverage the on-demand delivery infrastructure and customer base of the newly formed GoTo Group for food and grocery delivery.

E. The MSME Survey

To mitigate the lasting negative effects of the pandemic and identify ways to sustain MSMEs' growth, special attention should be given to their survival and resilience strategies, particularly the adoption of digital technology. In 2021, the Asian Development Bank (ADB) and Gojek undertook a joint study to examine the COVID-19 pandemic's impact in Indonesia on MSMEs in the food and beverage sector that sell and market their products on the GoFood platform. The study's objective was to gain a better understanding of the digitalization process among Indonesian MSMEs and explore their resilience during a long-lasting crisis such as the pandemic.

While a detailed account of the survey methodology is provided in Section II of this report, an overview is given here. The Gojek merchant survey comprised two stages (online and via phone), with a prior pilot survey for each stage to help optimize the coverage and clarity of survey questions. The online survey was conducted by Gojek and targeted GoFood merchants for voluntary survey participation from November to December 2021 in the highest and lowest revenue centers of GoFood. These were "Jabodetabek" (comprising Jakarta, Bogor, Depok, Tangerang, and Bekasi) and East Java, Bali, and East and West Nusa Tenggara, known collectively as "EJBN." The phone survey was conducted by the SMERU Research Institute from February to March 2022. This stage involved interviewing online survey participants who agreed to be contacted by phone to provide open-ended responses to a series of questions. Of the 869 GoFood merchants participating in the online survey, 375

agreed to be contacted for the phone survey, which had a participation rate of 73.3% (275 merchants).

The demographic profile of the MSME respondents to the online and phone surveys is presented in Section III. Participant data privacy was of paramount importance during the conduct of the surveys and the compilation of this summary report. Participation in the online survey was voluntary and responses were anonymized. Merchants' consent to participate was obtained before proceeding with the phone survey. The financial tokens of appreciation provided for participation in the surveys were deposited into participants' GoPay accounts, with all survey response data anonymized. Therefore, individual responses to phone survey questions that appear throughout this report include only general tracking characteristics (e.g., age, gender, number of employees, educational attainment, and location) and are not linked to the actual names of individual merchants.

The report's findings, which are discussed in detail in Section IV, rely primarily on the online survey data. The analysis is supplemented with phone responses and Gojek administrative data covering merchant information on date of registration with the platform, transactions, and routine operations. Phone survey responses reveal that Gojek had an important role in helping MSMEs maintain sufficient revenues during the pandemic. As noted by one survey participant:

> "I decided to sell my products online to expand my business. Orders from Gojek were pretty slow during the pandemic. But Gojek still helps to make my business survive."
>
> —Female respondent, 42 years old, EJBN, self-employed, high school education or higher.

Some survey respondents said that Gojek even helped facilitate the growth of their business during the pandemic by bringing in enough new online customers to account for decreased in-person sales:

> "GoFood helped to make my business survive and expand. Particularly, during the pandemic when no one was coming to my store. People stayed at home, shopped from home, so GoFood was helpful."
>
> —Female respondent, 43 years old, Jabodetabek, self-employed, high school education or higher.

Survey participants were appreciative of Gojek for providing access to a wider customer base through the GoFood app. At the same time, their responses provided insights into specific merchant concerns, as included in this section. This report's concluding observations in Section V are intended to highlight the opportunities to further support MSMEs in their economic recovery after the pandemic. In short, these observations emphasize the importance of resilience within the sector and the need for an inclusive recovery to be led by MSMEs that are well prepared for a more digital future.

II. Survey Methodology

A. Administrative Data

The analysis in this paper is based on two data sources: (i) weekly administrative and transactions data on all 288,296 GoFood merchants in Indonesia that were active on the platform as of February 2021; and (ii) primary data from an online survey and subsequent telephone survey conducted among GoFood merchants in two of the seven regions in Indonesia served by Gojek. The administrative data include information on merchant location, GoFood's new entrants and dropouts, consumer expenditures, and weekly revenues—as measured by GMV generated from online GoFood transactions.

This rich dataset covers the time period from 7 January 2019 to 28 February 2021, which has been further divided into seven subperiods for the purpose of analysis in this study. These subperiods were identified based on events that may have impacted MSMEs, such as the introduction of GoBiz platform services, spread of COVID-19, early phase of COVID-19, two lockdown periods when mobility was restricted, and lifting of these lockdowns, namely:

- Period 1 (P1), from 7 January to 30 June 2019, referred to as "Before COVID-19, before GoBiz" in this report;
- Period 2 (P2), from 1 July 2019 to 1 March 2020, i.e., "Before COVID-19, after GoBiz";
- Period 3 (P3), from 2 March to 5 April 2020, i.e., "Early COVID-19";
- Period 4 (P4), from 6 April to 5 July 2020, i.e., "First Lockdown";
- Period 5 (P5), from 6 July to 4 October 2020, i.e., "COVID-19 without Lockdown";
- Period 6 (P6), from 5 October to 6 December 2020, i.e., "Second Lockdown"; and
- Period 7 (P7), from 7 December 2020 to 28 February 2021, i.e., "After Second Lockdown."

B. Pilot Surveys

The online and phone survey questionnaires were jointly developed by Gojek and ADB. The objective of the pilot phase was to test the efficacy and clarity of the survey instruments. Based on feedback from the pilot surveys, the questionnaires were updated, and the enumerators were further trained before the full online and phone surveys were rolled out for implementation.

Gojek administered the pilot online survey by sending a SurveyMonkey link to targeted GoFood merchants for voluntary participation in April 2021. Each survey respondent was someone familiar with the business, including the business owner, manager, other staff, or the business owner's family members. The questions asked in the pilot online survey revolved around the pandemic's impact on sales and how using Gojek might have helped their MSME navigate the economic crisis. The link to the pilot survey was sent to 600 randomly selected GoFood merchants from seven regions representing the same geographic distribution as the entire population of GoFood merchants across Indonesia.

The survey link was sent to two groups of 300 merchants with different treatments. In Group 1, survey participants were informed that those who responded within 5 days would be paid an incentive of Rp100,000. Meanwhile, survey participants in Group 2 were told that those who responded within 8 days would be paid an incentive of Rp100,000. The incentive of Rp100,000 for completing the pilot online survey was around twice the standard rate that Gojek typically offers for its surveys. The response rate of 4.2% (25 out of 600 merchants) was about 2–3 times greater than what Gojek usually attains for its merchant surveys, likely a result of the enhanced incentive for participation.

In the pilot online survey, 13 merchants participated in Group 1. Of these 13 merchants, 12 received incentives, and 10 agreed to participate in the follow-up pilot phone survey. In Group 2, 12 merchants participated in the pilot online survey, and all of them received incentives. Meanwhile, 8 of the 12 merchants in Group 2 agreed to be contacted for the follow-up pilot phone survey.

Enumerators in the pilot phone survey collected data using Computer Assisted Personal Interview software, which was implemented with Survey Solutions, a data collection and survey management software. Interviews were recorded with the participants' permission. The interviews during the pilot phone survey typically lasted 15–30 minutes.

C. Online and Phone Surveys

The full online survey was carried out by Gojek in two phases in November–December 2021 among a random sample of 50,000 GoFood merchants in Jabodetabek and EJBN. These merchants represent GoFood's highest and lowest revenue-generating areas in Indonesia, respectively, as tracked through the GMV of all transactions during the study period. Further, the random sample selection reflected the actual percentages of all GoFood merchants operating in these two regions: about 65% of the surveyed merchants were from Jabodetabek and about 35% were from EJBN.

In the first phase, Gojek sent an online survey link to 25,000 merchants in November 2021. The number of merchants who participated in the first phase of the online survey was 753. Gojek sent the online survey link to another 25,000 merchants in early December 2021. The second phase garnered 116 additional responses, resulting in a total of 869 merchants participating in the online survey with a response rate of 1.7%. An incentive of Rp100,000 worth of GoPay vouchers was transferred to 25 responding merchants selected by lottery in each of the two phases of the online survey.

Online survey responses were deemed "of quality", i.e., respondents had answered the questions completely and mindfully, and included in the analyses if they passed the filters set up by the survey platform (SurveyMonkey) and Gojek Research Team. The filters included no speeding (filling in too fast) or a survey fill duration longer than 24 hours; no straight lining (only choosing certain orders in multiple choice questions, for example, selecting the first options for all questions. Furthermore, the order of response options was randomized during the survey to avoid order bias); no copy-and-pasting or nonsensical responses.

Of the 869 online survey participants, 375 agreed to be contacted for the follow-up phone survey. These 375 merchants were contacted by enumerators during the phone survey regardless of their online survey data quality and consistency. The survey team conducted the phone survey in two phases, lasting from 4 February to 25 March 2022, in which more detailed information related to the online survey questions was gathered. Of the 375 merchants who had previously agreed to be contacted for the follow-up phone survey, 275 (73.3%) participated in the phone survey. An incentive payment of Rp90,000 was transferred to each phone survey participant's GoPay account.

The phone survey sought comments on the pandemic's impact on the respondent's business and the role of digitalization in strengthening their MSME's resiliency or even enabling its growth. Phone interviews lasted for about 30–45 minutes on average, and captured merchants' comments and concerns, including expectations of support from the government and online platforms.

This report's findings are largely based on the analysis of quantitative online survey data supplemented by merchants' responses to questions in the phone survey, as well as administrative data from GoBiz, which serves as the "dashboard" for MSME owners using the GoFood app.[3] The location-based distribution of Gojek administrative data, online survey, and phone survey data used in this study are summarized in **Table 1**.

The survey dataset introduced gender-disaggregated data on MSME merchants as well as enterprise size data (by number of employees), which are not included in the administrative dataset. Thus, the two data sources complement one another and sharpen the analysis of merchants' income dynamics both before and during the pandemic.

Table 1: Gojek Administrative Database and the Surveys, Sample Distribution by Location

Business location	Gojek's administrative data	Online survey		Phone survey	
	%	n	%	n	%
Jabodetabek	65	562	64.70	169	63.80
EJBN	35	307	35.30	96	36.20

EJBN = East Java, Bali, and East and West Nusa Tenggara; Jabodetabek = Jakarta, Bogor, Depok, Tangerang, and Bekasi; n = sample size.
Sources: Online and phone surveys of GoFood merchants.

---

[3]   Survey findings are derived from the experiences of the GoFood merchants on the GoBiz platform.

III. Profile of GoFood MSMEs Surveyed

A. Demographic Overview of Survey Respondents

The online survey received responses from 869 GoFood merchants. However, not all survey questions were answered by merchants. The summary data in **Table 2** show that, of those who responded to the online survey, 13.7% skipped demographic questions, such as gender and education level, and 7.2% did not identify the number of employees in their businesses.

Table 2: Characteristics of Micro, Small, and Medium-Sized Enterprises Surveyed, Online Survey

Variable	Category	n	% or mean
Owner's gender	Female	270	31.1%
	Male	336	38.7%
	Joint	144	16.6%
	No response	119	13.7%
Respondent's role in business	Manager	25	2.9%
	Other staff	3	0.3%
	Owner	841	96.8%
Business size in March 2021	0 employee	446	51.3%
	1-4 employees	339	39.0%
	5-19 employees	18	2.1%
	More than 19 employees	3	0.3%
	No response	63	7.2%
Business location	Jabodetabek	562	64.7%
	EJBN	307	35.3%
Educational attainment	HS education or higher	629	72.4%
	Lower than HS	121	13.9%
	No response	119	13.7%
When business was established	Before pandemic	612	70.4%
	After pandemic	257	29.6%
When business joined GoFood platform	Before COVID-19, before GoBiz	151	17.4%
	Before COVID-19, after GoBiz	227	26.1%
	Early COVID-19	40	4.6%
	First lockdown	110	12.7%
	COVID-19 without lockdown	175	20.1%
	Second lockdown	120	13.8%
	After second lockdown	46	5.3%
GoFood GMV (in Rp)*		869	1,347,689
GoFood number of items*		869	66.7
GoFood number of transactions*		869	26.7

* = per merchant and per week, reported as mean; COVID-19 = coronavirus disease; EJBN = East Java, Bali, and East and West Nusa Tenggara; GMV = gross merchandise value; HS = high school; n = sample size; Rp = rupiah; Jabodetabek = Jakarta, Bogor, Depok, Tangerang, and Bekasi.

Note: "Joint" refers to enterprises jointly owned by more than one (male or female) merchant.

Sources: Online survey of GoFood merchants and Gojek's administrative database.

Among MSMEs that participated in the online survey, 38.7% were owned by males, while 31.1% were female-owned and 16.6% were jointly-owned (the remaining 13.7% did not provide a response to this survey question). More than half of the respondents were self-employed, with no employees (51.3%), and about two-thirds of all MSMEs were based in Jabodetabek (64.7%). Businesses established before the pandemic accounted for about 70% of MSMEs surveyed in this study. Around 72% of merchants who participated in the online survey had at least a high school education. Most of the online survey respondents were the business owner themselves (96.8%). Finally, of the seven periods introduced in Section II of this report, many of the MSMEs surveyed joined GoFood in the period "before COVID-19, after GoBiz" (26%), which corresponds to the time period from July 2019 to February 2020.

B. Length of Time on the GoFood App

In **Figure 1**, the length of time from the date a business joined GoFood until the date of the online survey in March 2021 is grouped under one of three categories: (i) "Since the spread of COVID-19" refers to businesses that joined GoFood between March 2020 and November 2021; (ii) "Between 1–3 years" refers to businesses that joined GoFood before the pandemic (March 2018–March 2020); and (iii) "More than 3 years" is defined as businesses that joined GoFood before March 2018.[4]

Approximately 36% of the MSMEs surveyed had already been on the GoFood platform for 1–3 years before the onset of the pandemic, while around 7% had been on the platform for more than 3 years. Therefore, around 56% joined GoFood during the pandemic. As the phone survey response below

---

4   Figure 1 was generated using the date of merchants' first transaction on GoFood platform, which is available in Gojek's administrative database.

Figure 1: Period when Micro, Small, and Medium-Sized Enterprises Joined GoFood Platform

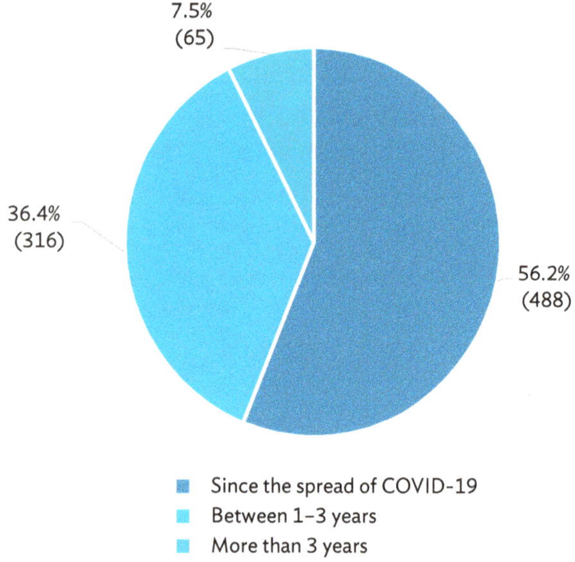

COVID-19 = coronavirus disease.
Note: Numbers in parentheses represent the total number of
           respondents for each category.
Sources: Online survey of GoFood merchants and Gojek's
           administrative database.

suggests, many merchants may have felt they had no choice but to seek an increase in online sales given the severe restrictions on mobility:

> "I used to sell my products offline, but I could no longer rely on selling offline, so I sell my products online now. Income from online sales rose around 30%."
>
> —Female respondent, 42 years old, EJBN, self-employed, high school education or higher.

Notably, those MSMEs that joined the platform before the pandemic had higher average GMV per transaction than those which joined during the pandemic, as shown in **Figure 2**. This suggests that some of the MSMEs which joined GoFood during the pandemic skewed toward those that may have simply been seeking to survive the crisis rather than to expand their business, though average GMV

per transaction steadily increased for both groups from subperiod 3 (Early COVID-19) to subperiod 7 (After second lockdown).

The likely explanation for the notable decline in sales after subperiod 1 (Before COVID-19, before GoBiz) is that this was the only period in which sales data were self-reported by the merchant. Following the introduction of GoBiz in 2019, actual sales data were recorded by Gojek. Transactions data were captured more accurately and comprehensively through platform-based tracking compared to self-reporting by merchants. Thus, the administrative data for subperiods 2–7 in Figure 2 more accurately reflect MSME sales than the self-reported data used for subperiod 1.

Self-employed MSMEs were more likely to start using GoFood during the pandemic. For some respondents, this was because they had recently lost employment, and therefore needed a new source of income, as cited by the following phone survey participant:

> "I started my business during the pandemic because I was laid off. So, I learned to open a business."
>
> —Male respondent, 56 years old, Jabodetabek, self-employed, high school education or higher.

C. Users of Multiple Online Platforms

Figure 3 presents the share of MSMEs using multiple online platforms.[5] More than 83% of MSMEs used Gojek and at least one other online platform, such as Grab or ShopeeFood, to operate their business. During the phone interviews, some merchants described a feeling of distress as their businesses confronted significant challenges in maintaining financial viability during the enforcement of

---

5   Figure 3 was generated using merchant responses to Question No. 16 in the online survey (see Appendix) and Gojek administrative database.

Figure 2: Average Gross Merchandise Value per Transaction, by Subperiod

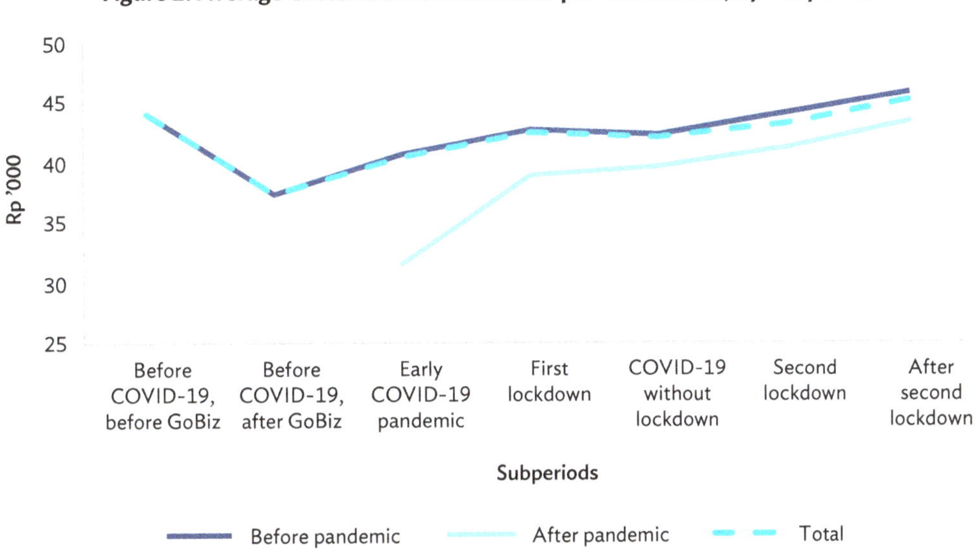

COVID-19 = coronavirus disease, Rp = rupiah.
Sources: Online survey of GoFood merchants and Gojek's administrative database.

pandemic-related mobility restrictions. While there may have been some individuals who were cautious to utilize several online platforms before the pandemic, the difficult economic situation compelled many MSMEs to explore other ways for generating income. As one MSME merchant said:

"I want to reach every customer who uses Gojek, Grab, and Shopee."

—Female respondent, 43 years old, Jabodetabek, 1–4 employees, high school education or higher.

Disaggregating the use of multiple online platforms by merchants' education level, **Figure 4** shows that merchants with at least a high school education tended to use more than one online platform more frequently than less educated merchants (85.2% vs. 73.5%).[6] This aligns with other findings that suggest the capacity for adoption of technology and financial literacy is generally higher among better educated individuals (Baihaqqy et al. 2020). Those with higher education would thus be

more equipped to take advantage of the different functionalities across the online platforms, as well as employ promotional schemes that better suit them.[7]

Figure 3: Online Platforms Used, by GoFood Merchants

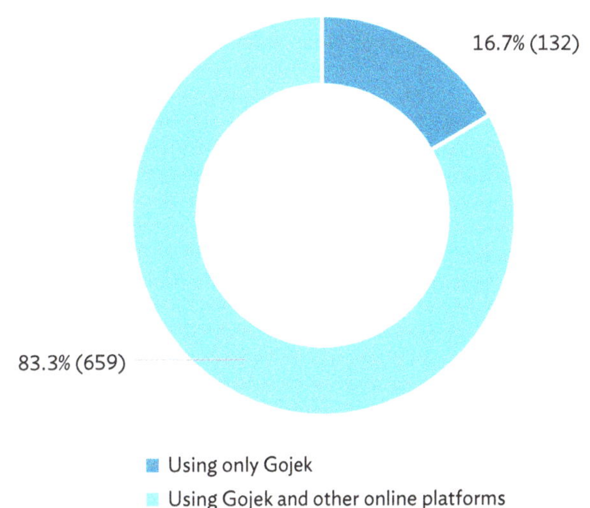

Note: Numbers in parentheses represent the total number of respondents for each category.
Sources: Phone survey of GoFood merchants and Gojek's administrative database.

---

6   Figure 4 was generated using merchant responses to Question Nos. 16 and 22 in the online survey (see Appendix) and Gojek administrative database.

7   Promotional schemes vary across platforms but often involve directing customer searches on the app to a particular restaurant and the placement of images of particular dishes alongside a menu. Thus, they generally increase the visibility of a particular restaurant or food service on the platform for a fee.

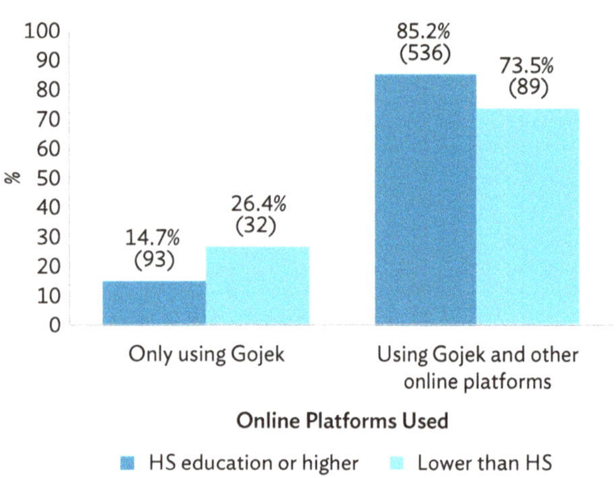

Figure 4: Online Platforms Used, by Merchant's Level of Education

HS = high school.
Note: Numbers in parentheses represent the total number of respondents for each category.
Sources: Online survey of GoFood merchants and Gojek's administrative database.

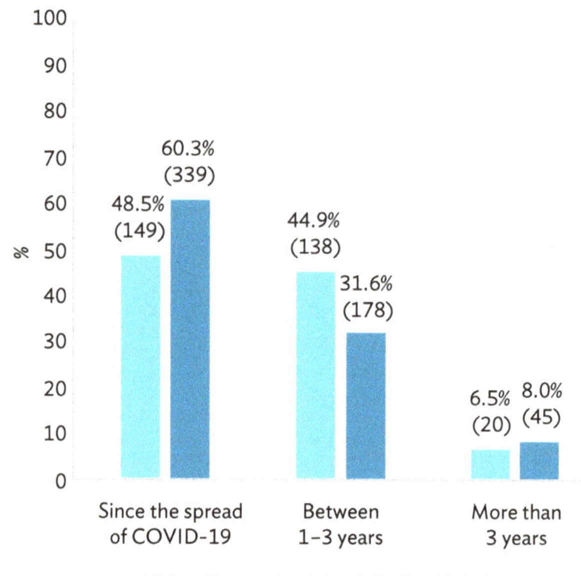

Figure 5: Period When Micro, Small, and Medium-Sized Enterprises Joined GoFood, by Location

COVID-19 = coronavirus disease; EJBN = East Java, Bali, and East and West Nusa Tenggara; Jabodetabek = Jakarta, Bogor, Depok, Tangerang, and Bekasi.
Note: Numbers in parentheses represent the total number of respondents for each category.
Sources: Online survey of GoFood merchants and Gojek's administrative database.

D. Regional Differences between MSMEs in EJBN and Jabodetabek

Figure 5 highlights the difference between EJBN and Jabodetabek in terms of when merchants in these regions joined GoFood.[8] More than 60% of MSMEs in Jabodetabek that were using GoFood in March 2021 had joined the platform since the onset of the pandemic a year earlier. This compares with 48.5% of MSMEs in EJBN. The discrepancy is likely the result of tighter mobility restrictions in Jabodetabek, particularly in Jakarta. The restrictions pushed customers to purchase more food online since in-person dining options were severely curtailed (Badan Pemeriksa Keuangan 2020). In response to this shift in demand, many merchants in Jabodetabek who had not previously used an app as part of their business operations joined online platforms such as Gojek to expand their reach and maintain sales during the pandemic.

E. MSME Size and Ownership by Gender

As seen in Table 2 in Section III, more than half (51.3%) of MSMEs respondents of the online survey had no employees—that is, a business operated solely by the owner. With relatively less income, human capital, and financial resources even before the onset of COVID-19, self-employed MSMEs were at a disadvantage in the face of an unpredictable event like the COVID-19 pandemic and therefore had a higher likelihood of experiencing income losses, particularly in terms of online sales. Disaggregating MSME ownership by gender, 38.7%, 31.1%, and 16.6% of MSMEs participating in the online survey were male-owned, female-owned, and jointly

---

[8]   Figure 5 was generated using merchant responses to Question No. 15 in the online survey (see Appendix) and Gojek administrative database.

owned, respectively. Gender-disaggregated data on the distinct pandemic experiences of male MSME owners as opposed to female MSME owners will be examined more closely in the next section.

F. Insights for Future Surveys

The online and phone surveys produced valuable data that complemented Gojek's already comprehensive administrative database. Specifically, the surveys added two key pieces of information about Gojek merchants: (i) size of the business, as measured by the number of employees; and (ii) whether a business is owned by a male, female, or jointly by males and females. With these two additional data points, the Gojek–ADB research team was able to compare how the pandemic affected MSMEs differently, based on their size, and the gender of their owner.

There were some discrepancies between merchants' responses to the same question in the online survey and the subsequent phone survey. This could be explained by the enumerator clarifying a merchant's previous response in the online survey, or by changes in MSMEs' business situation between the time of the online survey and the subsequent phone interview.

Table 3 summarizes the profiles of merchants who participated in both surveys, illustrating some of the discrepancies between merchant responses to the online survey and the phone survey. For example, in the phone survey, fewer merchants reported that their business was owned by a female than in the online survey: 63 of 275 (22.9%) in the phone survey compared with 80 of 275 (29.0%) in the online survey. In addition, more merchants indicated that their business was jointly owned in the phone survey than they did in the online survey: 90 of 275 (32.7%) vs. 54 of 275 (19.6%), respectively.

There may also have been a selection bias issues related to merchants' decisions to participate in the surveys. It is possible that the relatively more successful and established merchants were more likely to respond to the surveys. On the other hand, some merchants who were less satisfied with the app may also have been driven to participate in the survey to offer feedback to Gojek, with possible oversampling of different ends of the spectrum in terms of satisfaction with the GoFood app.

In addition, merchants from only two of the seven Indonesian regions in which GoFood operates were surveyed, with these two regions representing the online platform's highest and lowest revenue-generating areas (in terms of GMV). Hence, survey findings pertain specifically to these two regions and further investigation would be warranted before the findings may be extended to the entire GoFood merchant population in Indonesia.

The response rate to the full online survey was 1.7%, i.e., less than half of the 4.2% response rate for the pilot survey. The fact that the incentive payment of Rp100,000 was only given to 25 randomly selected respondents—rather than to all respondents who completed their survey by the assigned deadline—may have contributed to the low response rate for the full online survey.

The surveys also revealed procedural takeaways for future similar efforts. A review of the phone survey transcripts revealed that a good portion of each interview was spent clarifying the questions being asked of merchants. In some cases, merchants faced challenges in allocating time to respond to interviewers, while also managing their MSMEs. In addition, an official endorsement of the survey from a recognized source—such as the Gojek platform itself—helped assure potential respondents of the survey's credibility and likely led to an improved response rate.

Table 3: Characteristics of Micro, Small, and Medium-Sized Enterprises Surveyed, Online and Phone Surveys

Variable	Category	Phone survey respondents		Online survey respondents**	
		n	%	n	% or mean
Owner's gender	Female	63	22.9%	80	29.1%
	Male	122	44.4%	141	51.3%
	Joint	90	32.7%	54	19.6%
Respondent's role in business	Owner	258	93.8%	266	96.7%
	Manager	13	4.7%	9	3.3%
	Other staff	4	1.5%	0	0.0%
Business size in March 2021	0 employee	78	28.4%	145	52.7%
	1–4 employees	177	64.4%	122	44.4%
	5–19 employees	14	5.1%	8	2.9%
	More than 19 employees	1	0.4%	0	0%
	No response	5	1.8%	0	0%
Business location	Jabodetabek	176	64.0%	179	65.1%
	EJBN	99	36.0%	96	34.9%
Educational attainment	HS education or higher	233	84.7%	237	86.2%
	Lower than HS	36	13.1%	38	13.8%
	No response	6	2.2%	0	0.0%
When business was established	Before pandemic	205	74.5%	198	72.0%
	After pandemic	70	25.5%	77	28.0%
When business joined GoFood	Before COVID-19, before GoBiz (P1)	50	18.2%	50	18.2%
	Before COVID-19, after GoBiz (P2)	64	23.3%	64	23.3%
	Early COVID-19 (P3)	18	6.5%	18	6.5%
	First lockdown (P4)	35	12.7%	35	12.7%
	COVID-19 without lockdown (P5)	53	19.3%	53	19.3%
	Second lockdown (P6)	39	14.2%	39	14.2%
	After second lockdown (P7)	16	5.8%	16	5.8%
GoFood GMV (in Rp)*				275	1,114,939
GoFood number of items*				275	67.9
GoFood number of transactions*				275	27.9

* = per merchant and per week, reported as mean; ** = online survey respondents who have also participated in the phone survey; COVID-19 = coronavirus disease; EJBN = East Java, Bali, and East and West Nusa Tenggara; GMV = gross merchandise value; HS = high school; Jabodetabek = Jakarta, Bogor, Depok, Tangerang, and Bekasi; n = sample size; P = subperiod; Rp = rupiah.

Notes: GoFood GMV (in Rp), GoFood number of items sold, and GoFood number of transactions are indicated per merchant per week and they are the same for phone and online surveys. The number of observations for these variables are extracted from Gojek administrative database. "Joint" refers to enterprises jointly owned by more than one (male or female) merchant.

Sources: Online and phone surveys of GoFood merchants and Gojek administrative database.

IV. Findings of the Study

A. The Pandemic's Impact on the Indonesian MSME Sector

The COVID-19 pandemic weighed heavily on the food and beverage sector in Indonesia, particularly on the MSMEs. Output in the sector contracted by 16.8% in the second quarter of 2020 (Statistics Indonesia 2020). The economy then struggled to recover during the second half of the year. The relaxation on mobility restrictions in the fourth quarter reinvigorated the virus' spread but failed to revitalize private consumption. With COVID-19 infections and deaths reaching record numbers in January 2021, the government had little choice but to implement a second lockdown, which had an initial adverse effect on the economy (Al Jazeera 2021). However, by the end of 2021, the economy began to recover (ADB 2022).

As one phone survey participant noted about her business amid the pandemic:

> "Income from online sales dropped drastically because only a few customers were ordering my food then. The income dropped up to 70% (from March 2020 to March 2021). Sometimes, I did not get a single order at all in a day."
>
> —Female respondent, 34 years old, Jabodetabek, self-employed, high school education or higher.

This section reviews the survey data to determine the share of MSMEs that experienced gains, losses, or no change in online and offline sales, as well as how the specific characteristics of a business (e.g., size, location, and merchant's educational attainment) might have affected the MSME's pandemic experience. Also included in this section are discussions of the (i) factors that drove merchants to borrow (or not borrow) from banks, friends and family, and other sources; (ii) role of public assistance in supporting MSMEs during the pandemic; and (iii) differences in pandemic impacts and coping strategies between female- and male-owned MSMEs.

B. Assessing Changes in MSMEs' Income through the Gojek Survey

The MSME survey undertaken in 2021 by Gojek and ADB assessed three kinds of changes in income among GoFood users in Indonesia: (i) change in overall revenue (i.e., from offline and online sales); (ii) change in revenue from offline sales; and (iii) change in revenue from online sales. **Figure 6** shows the shares of MSMEs experiencing a gain in revenue, a loss of revenue, or no change in revenue between March 2020 and February 2021.[9] A loss in revenue from all sales was reported by 73.4% of MSME respondents, while 74.6% of surveyed MSMEs reported losses in offline sales, and 59.4% of MSMEs suffered losses in online sales. As expected, declining revenue among MSMEs was less widespread for online sales than offline sales. During both lockdowns that occurred in the review period from March 2020 to March 2021, physical stores and restaurants were closed, and many merchants had no other option but to sell their products online—an approach that some were poised to pursue more aggressively. In fact, over 40% of MSMEs reported increased online sales between March 2020 and February 2021, compared with only 21.3% reporting similar gains for offline sales.

Online food service delivery platforms such as GoFood were instrumental in enabling merchants to reach their existing customers and, in many instances, identify new ones. This helped

---

9   Figure 6 was generated using merchant responses to Question Nos. 10 and 11 in the online survey (see Appendix) and Gojek administrative database.

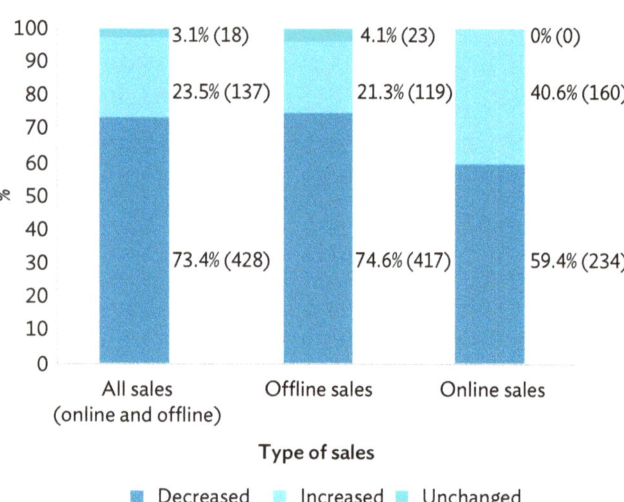

Figure 6: Change in Revenue during the Pandemic, by Type of Sales

MSMEs = micro, small, and medium-sized enterprises.
Notes: Change in revenue from March 2020 to February 2021. The total number of MSMEs that experienced changes in revenue from online and offline sales (583 MSMEs), from only offline sales (559 MSMEs), and from only online sales (394 MSMEs) vary. Hence, relative percentages within each group are shown above. Numbers in parentheses represent the total number of respondents for each category.
Sources: Online survey of GoFood merchants and Gojek's administrative database.

a critical mass of Indonesian MSMEs to maintain enough income to survive the pandemic. A common sentiment conveyed by many merchants in their phone interviews was an appreciation of the presence of online platforms during such a challenging time. Transcripts from phone interviews reveal that participants often recognized Gojek's role during the pandemic, by using terms such as "helpful," "really helpful," and "very helpful."

C. Regional Differences in Impact

As discussed in Section II, the survey sample comprised MSMEs located in two distinct regions of Indonesia, i.e., Jabodetabek and EJBN. **Figure 7** shows sales gains and losses for MSMEs from March 2020 to February 2021 based on their location, revealing that MSMEs in EJBN were more likely to experience a decline in online income compared with those in Jabodetabek (62.2% vs. 57.6%), while offline sales fell more for MSMEs in Jabodetabek (76.7% vs. 71.0%).[10]

Figure 7: Change in Revenue during the Pandemic, by Location and Type of Sales

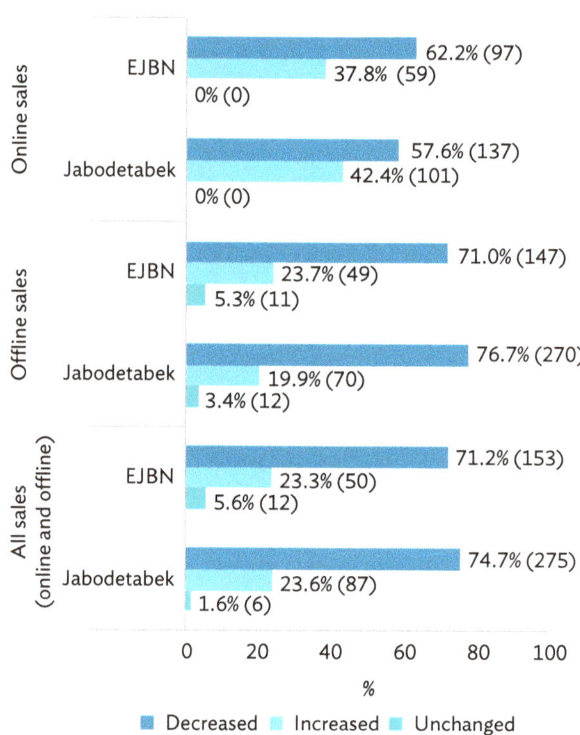

EJBN = East Java, Bali, and East and West Nusa Tenggara;
Jabodetabek = Jakarta, Bogor, Depok, Tangerang, and Bekasi;
MSMEs = micro, small, and medium-sized enterprises.
Notes: Change in revenue from March 2020 to February 2021. Numbers in parentheses represent the total number of respondents for each category.
Sources: Online survey of GoFood merchants and Gojek's administrative data.

---

10   Figure 7 was generated using merchant responses to Question Nos. 10 and 11 in the online survey (see Appendix) and Gojek administrative database.

These findings may reflect in-person business activity being more severely curtailed in the more densely populated areas of Jabodetabek during the pandemic. Further, the relatively stronger reliance on food service delivery platforms among MSMEs located in metropolitan areas—once again due to population density—may have also better prepared them for the pandemic-induced shift to online sales. Meanwhile, MSMEs located in less densely populated areas may have been at a disadvantage in terms of delivering food to customers, given the greater distances required for pickup and delivery. Some respondents to the phone survey from EJBN also suggested that the nonavailability of delivery riders in less densely populated locations was a significant problem at times during the pandemic:

> "I would like them to add to the number of drivers in my region. Actually, I have a lot of orders, but there are no drivers after 9 p.m."

> —Male respondent, 26 years old, EJBN, 1–4 employees, high school education or higher.

D. Merchant's Educational Attainment and Pandemic Experience

Figure 8 presents the shares of MSMEs which experienced a change in revenue from March 2020 to February 2021 based on merchants' level of education.[11] Declines in offline sales during the pandemic were experienced roughly equally by MSMEs headed by a merchant with at least a high school education and those headed by a merchant without a high school education (74.9% vs. 76.8%,

respectively). However, 61.6% of MSMEs headed by a merchant with at least a high school education saw a decline in online sales during the pandemic compared to only 50.8% for MSMEs headed by someone without a high school education.

Figure 8: Change in Revenue during the Pandemic, by Merchant's Level of Education and Type of Sales

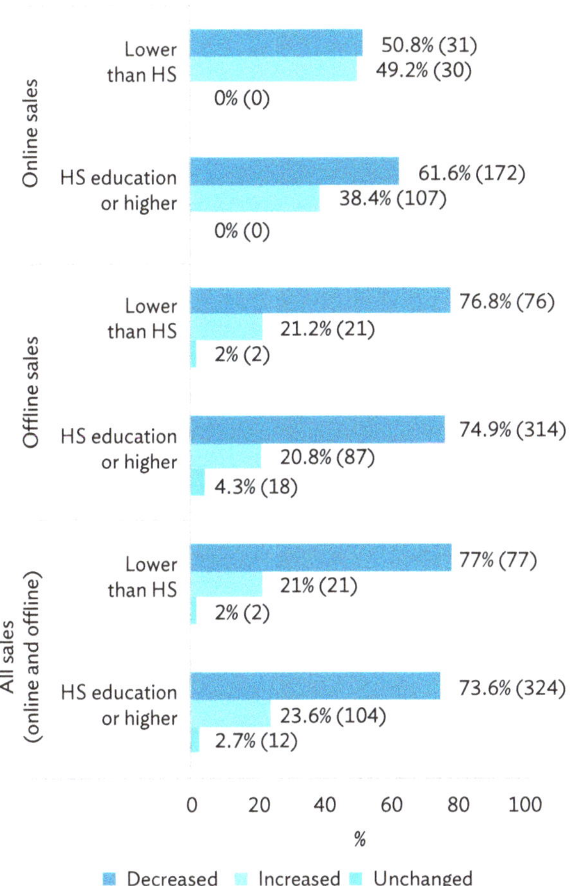

HS = high school; MSMEs = micro, small, and medium-sized enterprises.
Notes: Change in revenue from March 2020 to February 2021. The total number of MSMEs that experienced changes in revenue by respondents' educational attainment vary (for all sales, 540 MSMEs; for offline sales, 518 MSMEs; for online sales, 340 MSMEs). Hence, relative percentages within each group are shown. Numbers in parentheses represent the total number of respondents for each category.
Sources: Online survey of GoFood merchants and Gojek's administrative database.

---

11   Figure 8 was generated using merchant responses to Question Nos. 10, 11, and 22 in the online survey (see Appendix) and Gojek administrative database.

While this finding might seem to contradict the assertion that successful technology utilization is more common among those with higher education (Riddell and Song 2012), there may be another explanation. As shown in **Figure 9**, the average weekly GMV for MSMEs headed by individuals with at least a high school education exceeded the average weekly GMV for MSMEs headed by those without a high school education in all seven periods covered by the study. Meanwhile, among MSMEs led by a merchant with at least a high school education, 25.8% experienced a decline in average weekly GMV from March 2020 to March 2021, compared with only 14.8% of MSMEs led by someone without a high school education. Therefore, the steeper declines in average weekly GMV that were experienced by MSMEs headed by better educated merchants might have been the result of these average weekly GMVs having more room to fall from their relatively higher pre-pandemic levels.[12]

Figure 10 shows the various strategies that MSMEs utilized to cope with the negative economic impacts of the pandemic by the merchants' level of education (survey question nos. 12 and 22 in the Appendix). Such coping strategies included, but were not limited to: spending less on food, clothes, and leisure; pawning assets; reducing communication expenses; and not seeing a doctor while sick. The coping strategies of merchants with at least a high school education and those without a high school education varied. It is possible that merchants with a higher level of education might have had more situational awareness about the course of the pandemic in Indonesia and therefore were more likely to adopt mitigating and coping measures in response. However, all merchants, regardless of educational attainment, would have been affected by the pandemic's negative economic impacts. A higher disposable income may be another explanation, with better-educated merchants (compared with less-educated merchants) opting to use multiple coping

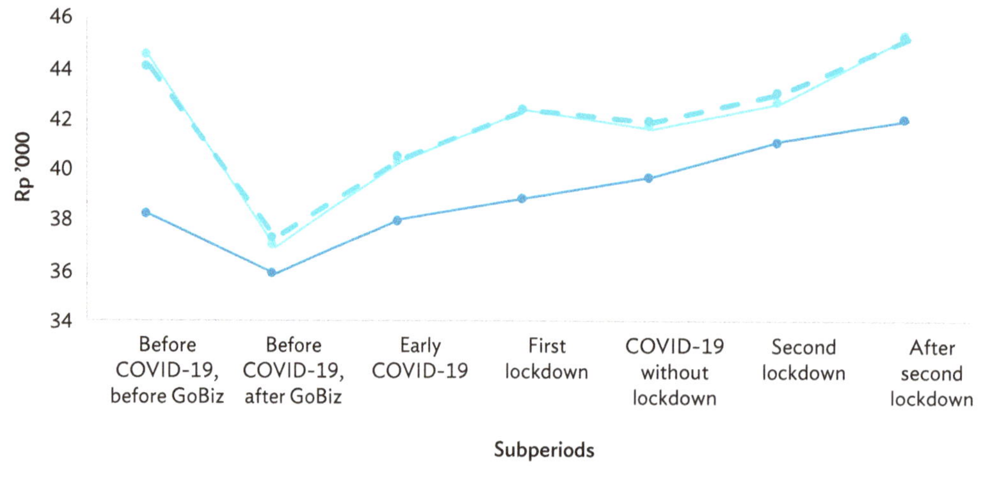

Figure 9: Average Gross Merchandise Value per Transaction, by Subperiod and Level of Education

COVID-19 = coronavirus disease; HS = high school; P = subperiod; Rp = rupiah.
Note: The number of observations in P1=130, P2=325, P3=344, P4=442, P5=595, P6=688, P7=750.
Sources: Online survey of GoFood merchants and Gojek's administrative database.

---

[12]   Figure 9 was generated using merchant responses to Question No. 22 in the online survey (see Appendix) and Gojek administrative database. While the average weekly GMV include both online and offline sales, Gojek's transaction data indicate that MSMEs earned most of their income from online sales during the pandemic.

measures when faced with falling revenues. These MSMEs would have had more capacity to decrease what were considered to be nonessential expenses or to reasonably reduce essential expenses.

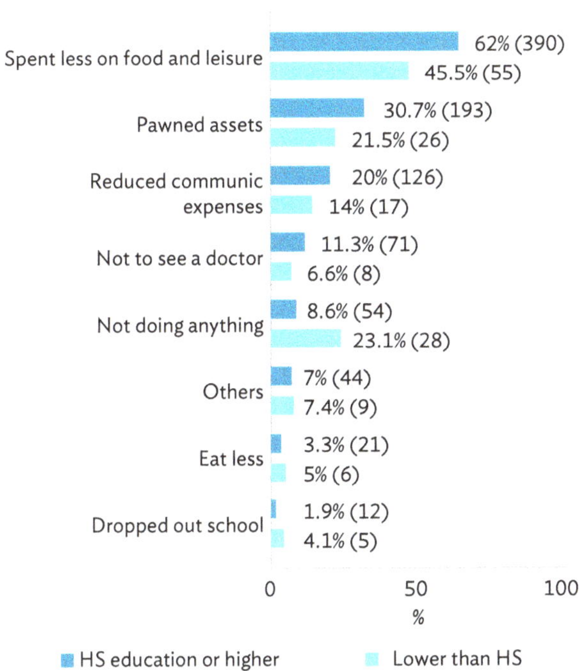

Figure 10: Pandemic Coping Strategies, by Level of Education

HS = high school.
Notes: Coping strategies in the period between March 2020 (beginning of the pandemic) to February 2021. Numbers in parentheses represent the total number of respondents for each category.
Source: Online survey of GoFood merchants.

The survey also revealed that there was greater employee churn during the pandemic among MSMEs headed by merchants with at least a high school education. MSMEs in this category were more likely to both downsize their business by reducing the number of employees and to expand their business size by taking on more employees compared to merchants with less educational attainment.

Figure 11 depicts the share of MSMEs experiencing a change in business size during the pandemic by the merchants' educational attainment. It reveals that 5.7% of MSMEs headed by merchants with at least a high school education reduced their number of employees between March 2020 and March 2021, compared with 4.0% of merchants without a high school education (Survey Question Nos. 7, 8, and 22 in the Appendix). Figure 11 also shows that a higher proportion of merchants with at least a high school education (6.6%) upsized their business during the pandemic compared to merchants without a high school education (5.0%).

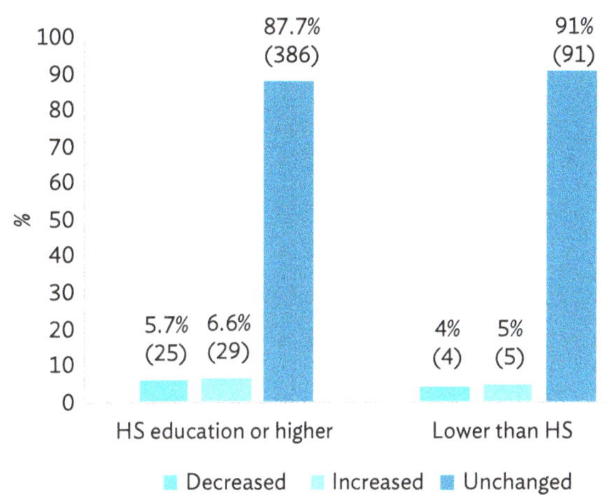

Figure 11: Change in Business Size during the Pandemic, by Level of Education

HS = high school.
Notes: Change in business size from March 2020 to March 2021. Numbers in parentheses represent the total number of respondents for each category.
Source: Online survey of GoFood merchants.

These dual observations reflect more dynamic business activity during the pandemic, as measured by retrenchment and expansion, among MSMEs headed by better educated merchants.

E. Income Losses and Downsizing by Business Size

As shown in **Figure 12**, 67% of self-employed MSMEs, i.e., MSMEs with no employees, suffered a decrease in online sales during the pandemic, compared with 52.4% of MSMEs with 1–4 employees, and 60.0% of MSMEs with 5–19 employees.[13] It may indicate that increased household responsibilities during lockdown periods—such as childcare, homeschooling, and caregiving—drew self-employed merchants' time and attention away from business operations, particularly for women-owned MSMEs. MSMEs operated solely by the owner may also have faced more challenges in applying digital technology to business processes during the pandemic since they did not have any employees to support these efforts.

Figure 13 presents the proportion of MSMEs that experienced a change in their business size, as measured by the number of employees, during the pandemic (Survey Question Nos. 7 and 8 in the Appendix). Despite nearly three-quarters of all surveyed MSMEs reporting declining sales between March 2020 and February 2021 (Figure 7), 9 out of 10 MSMEs were able to avoid reducing their number of employees. More than half (53.7%) tapped into their personal savings, often to financially support their employees:

"We use our savings to pay employees' salaries rather than cut their payments. [We] have to do this because we think about the people who work here, no matter how hard it is for us."

—Male respondent, 35 years old, Jabodetabek, 5–19 employees, high school education or higher.

Figure 12: Change in Revenue during the Pandemic, by Number of Employees and Type of Sales

Notes: Change in revenue from March 2020 to February 2021. Business size refers to the business size in March 2021. The total number of micro, small, and medium-sized enterprises (MSMEs) that experienced changes in revenue by business size vary (for all sales, 583 MSMEs; for offline sales, 599 MSMEs; for online sales, 368 MSMEs). Numbers in parentheses represent the total number of respondents for each category.
Sources: Online survey of GoFood merchants and Gojek's administrative database.

---

13   Figure 12 was generated using merchant responses to Question No. 7 in the online survey (see Appendix) and Gojek administrative database.

Figure 13: Change in Business Size during the Pandemic

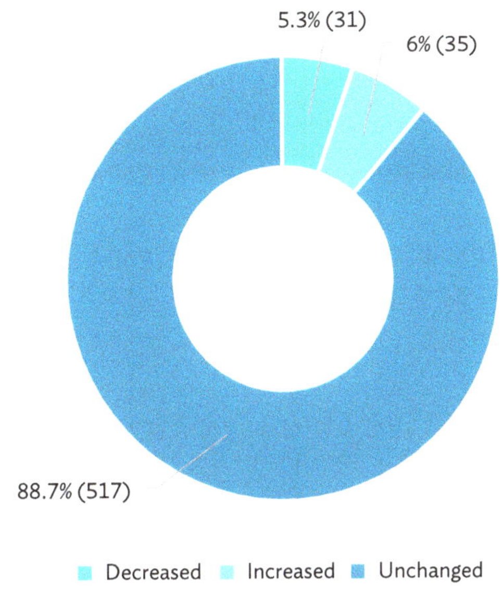

Notes: Change in business size from March 2020 to March 2021.
           Numbers in parentheses represent the total number of
           respondents for each category.
Source: Online survey of GoFood merchants.

Figure 14: Change in Business Size during the Pandemic, by Number of Employees

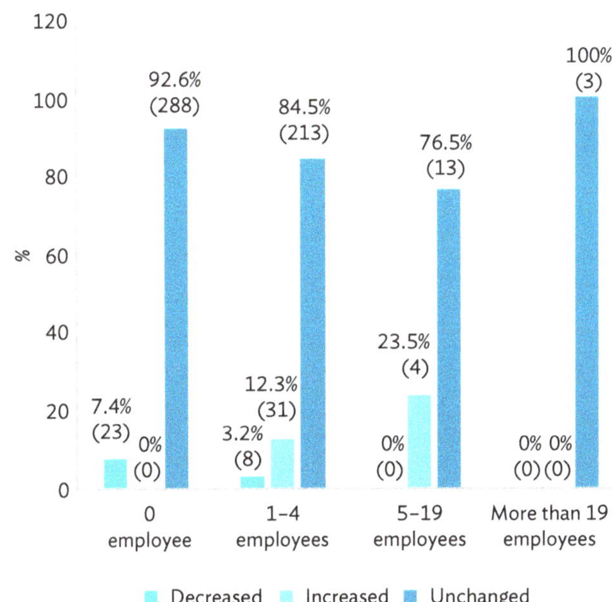

Notes: Change in business size from March 2020 to March 2021.
           Business size refers to business size in March 2021.
           Numbers in parentheses represent the total number of
           respondents for each category.
Source: Online survey of GoFood merchants.

However, in other cases, the owner or operator of an MSME may have felt compelled to let staff go to reduce expenses in order to survive the pandemic. This appears to have been most likely to occur among micro-sized enterprises. **Figure 14** compares MSMEs of varied sizes (self-employed with zero employees, micro with 1–4 employees, small with 5–19 employees, and medium with more than 19 employees). It reveals that 7.4% of MSMEs with zero employees as of March 2021 had reduced the number of their employees during the previous 12 months (Survey Question Nos. 7 and 8 in the Appendix). Among businesses with 1–4 employees as of March 2021, 3.2% experienced a reduction of employees during the pandemic, while none of the small-sized businesses (with 5–19 employees) surveyed had reduced the number of their employees in the preceding year. Phone survey data further revealed that some of these merchants replaced a salaried employee with an unsalaried family member or friend as a means of cost-cutting.

A modest share of MSMEs managed to increase their employee numbers during the pandemic, once again reflecting their role as engines of employment generation in Indonesia. For MSMEs with 1–4 employees as of March 2021, 12.3% experienced an increase in the number of employees in the prior year; for MSMEs with 5–19 employees, this share was 23.5%.[14]

F. To Borrow or Not to Borrow

More than half of all surveyed merchants reported using their personal savings to cope with the financial hardship unleashed by the pandemic. **Figure 15** shows sources of financing used by GoFood MSMEs during the pandemic (Survey Question No. 13 in the Appendix). Compared with the utilization of personal savings, a relatively small

---

14   MSMEs with zero employees as of March 2021 were not included in this part of the discussion because they could not have increased the number of their employees in the prior 12 months, while MSMEs with more than 19 employees were excluded due to small sample size of three survey respondents.

Figure 15: Sources of Financing

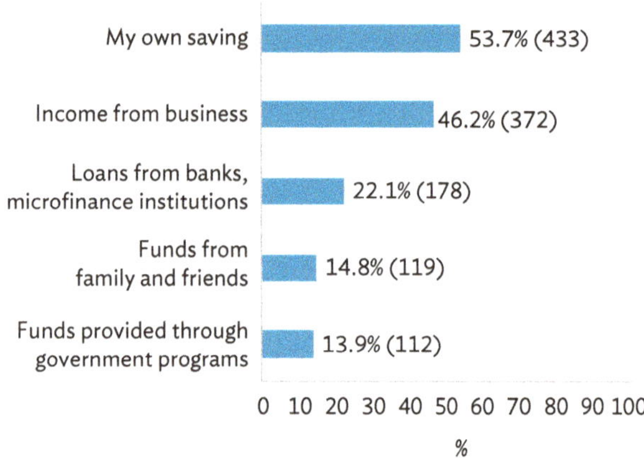

Notes: Sources of financing for GoFood merchants between March 2020 (beginning of the pandemic) to February 2021. Numbers in parentheses represent the total number of respondents for each category.
Source: Online survey of GoFood merchants.

percentage of merchants took out a loan from a financial institution (22.1%), which might otherwise be viewed as a potentially useful source of financing during a difficult period.

MSMEs established before the pandemic were more likely to get loans from financial institutions (25.4%) than those established during the pandemic (14.2%) (Amelia et al. 2022). This is not surprising as older firms would have a more established financial track record and thus access to funding, if not also a greater awareness of financing options. Meanwhile, MSMEs established after the pandemic were more likely to obtain funds from family and friends.

According to Japhta et al. (2016), the main reasons that MSMEs typically do not borrow from financial institutions, especially banks, are high-interest rates, complicated procedures, and onerous collateral requirements. In the Indonesian context, this hesitancy to take out a loan was expressed by several phone survey participants, including the following:

"No, never. Since COVID-19 started, I don't want to take out any loans. I don't want to burden myself."

—Female respondent, 54 years old, EJBN, 1–4 employees, high school education or higher.

For other Indonesian merchants, religious considerations—specifically, the prohibition against usury—was the primary factor in not seeking a loan:

"Thank God, 100% of the capital in my business is from the profit. In my business, there is no such thing as a loan. In doing business, I avoid usury. Because I'm a Muslim, so I want to run my business in a *halal* way, and it will be a blessing."

—Female respondent, 26 years old, Jabodetabek, more than 19 employees, high school education or higher.

Recognizing that many MSMEs are unlikely to meet a commercial bank's stringent criteria for a loan and that a typical bank's disbursal timelines are not suitable for MSMEs in need of immediate capital, Gojek began offering working capital loans to its merchant partners in 2018. By 2020, the GoBiz app was able to automatically track a business' GoFood revenue and easily determine its repayment capacity for an infusion of pre-approved working capital in the range of Rp1.5 million ($90) to Rp150 million ($9,000), with repayment periods of 2–12 months.[15] This arrangement makes the disbursal and recovery of payments relatively easy. From March 2020 to February 2021, 11.2% of surveyed MSMEs used GoModal.

---

15   The discussion on GoModal in this section was derived from Rajmohan (2020).

G. Government Assistance for MSMEs during the Pandemic

As shown in **Figure 15**, only 13.9% of surveyed MSMEs relied upon government-sponsored financial support for business financing during the pandemic. Further, **Figure 16** reveals that nearly half (47.5%) of survey respondents did not avail of any public assistance from March 2020 to February 2021 (Survey Question No. 14 in the Appendix). A combination of factors is responsible for the relatively limited reach of public assistance programs in Indonesia during the pandemic, including a lack of awareness of such programs among potential beneficiaries and extended application processes.

Phone survey respondents cited their frustration with social assistance application procedures, which may have seemed confusing or otherwise too onerous for some merchants:

"I never received any government assistance program (during the pandemic). I kept trying to apply for the program but always failed. I applied for *Prakerja* Card program but did not get it. I don't know why, it's beyond me."

—Female respondent, 29 years old, EJBN, self-employed, high school education or higher.

Other respondents cited inefficiency in the delivery of public assistance that may have been partially due to incomplete or outdated information on the status of MSMEs, at a time when data collection and verification were particularly challenging:

"The government does not distribute the assistance program, like business capital, for MSMEs equally. From what I know, the majority of the people who received that assistance don't run their businesses. The ones that run their own business mostly didn't get the assistance because the government still uses the old data."

—Male respondent, 31 years old, Jabodetabek, 1–4 employees, less than high school education.

Figure 16: Government Support Received during the Pandemic by GoFood Merchants

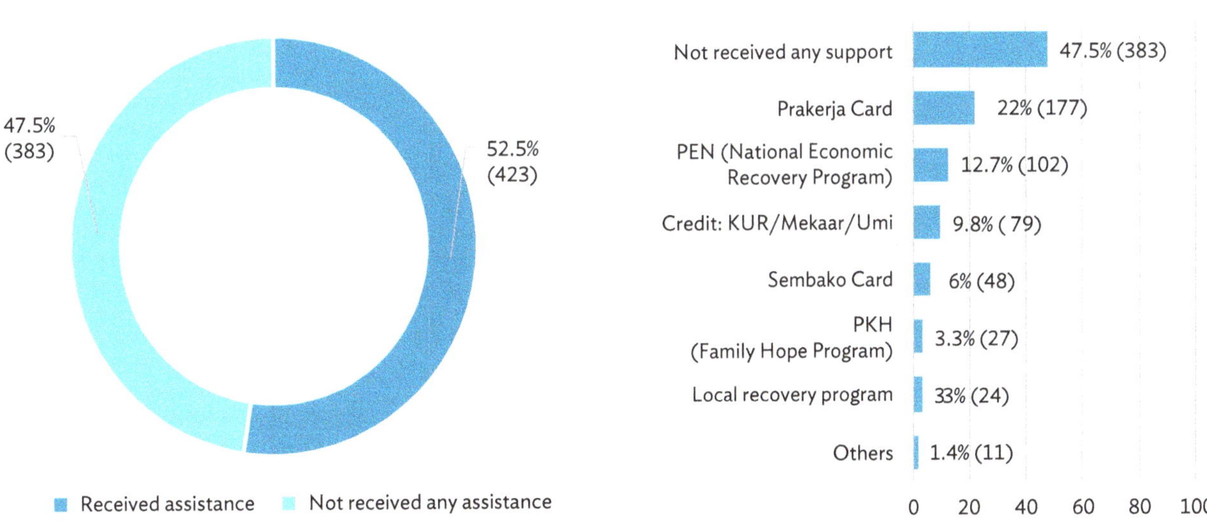

KUR = *Kredit Usaha Rakyat*, PEN = *Pemulihan Ekonomi Nasional*, PKH = *Program Keluarga Harapan*.
Notes: Government support programs received by enterprise between March 2020 (the beginning of the pandemic) to February 2021.
    Numbers in parentheses represent the total number of respondents for each category.
Source: Online survey of GoFood merchants.

Such feedback from survey participants aligns with findings from studies on Indonesian public assistance programs, which concluded that insufficient coordination in beneficiary data collection and management prevented many poor and vulnerable people from receiving needed assistance during the initial stages of the pandemic.[16]

MSMEs located in EJBN benefited less from support programs during the pandemic than those located in Jabodetabek, with 52.7% of MSMEs in EJBN failing to receive any government assistance compared with 44.7% in Jabodetabek. Many MSMEs in Jakarta also benefited from local government support programs, such as cash transfer schemes, that were made available exclusively for Jakarta-based businesses (DKI Jakarta Provincial Government 2021). Thus, while government assistance programs provided a lifeline to MSMEs during the pandemic, additional awareness building efforts and distribution measures were required to ensure all MSMEs could access such support regardless of their location in the country.

Figure 17 presents the share of MSMEs or individuals receiving one of several types of government assistance from March 2020 to February 2021, by whether or not their MSME experienced an increase or decrease in online sales.[17] The figure highlights that among survey participants there was no correlation between MSMEs' increased (or decreased) income during the pandemic and whether they received assistance via any government support programs. Yet more than 85% of surveyed households in Indonesia received social assistance from Indonesia's PEN Program during the first year of the pandemic (UNICEF 2021). Thus, government support did likely help some of the most vulnerable MSME owners by ameliorating the impact of lost income due to the restrictions on mobility.

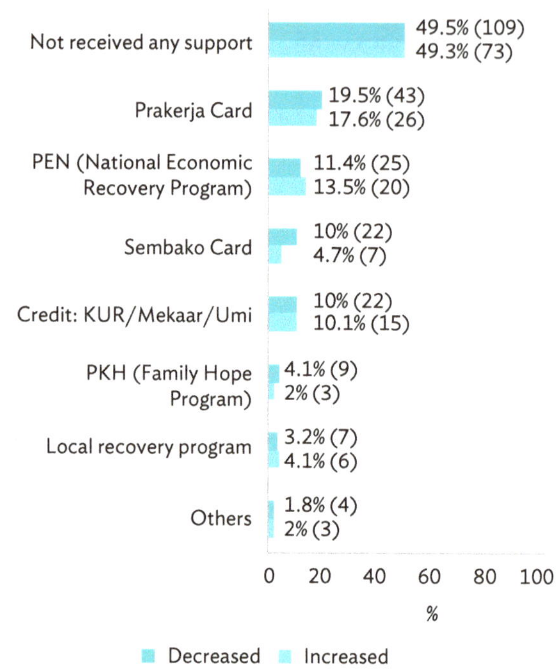

Figure 17: Government Support Received during the Pandemic, by Program and Change in Online Sales

KUR = *Kredit Usaha Rakyat*, PEN = *Pemulihan Ekonomi Nasional*, PKH = *Program Keluarga Harapan*.
Notes: Government support programs received by enterprises between March 2020 (the beginning of the pandemic) to February 2021. Change in income from March 2020 to February 2021. Numbers in parentheses represent the total number of respondents for each category.
Sources: Online survey of GoFood merchants and Gojek's administrative database.

Figure 18 shows the share of MSMEs (or individuals) that received public assistance by whether they experienced a change in business size between March 2020 to March 2021 (Survey Question Nos. 7, 8, and 14). It offers potential evidence of the positive impact of public assistance on MSMEs during the pandemic. It shows that merchants who did not have to reduce their number of employees during the pandemic were more likely to have received assistance during the pandemic from programs such as Prakerja Card, PEN, and Sembako Card, or from other local government

---

¹⁶ See, for example, SMERU Research Institute (2020).

¹⁷ Figure 17 was generated using merchant responses to Question No. 14 in the online survey (see Appendix) and Gojek administrative database.

Figure 18: Government Support Received during the Pandemic, by Change in Business Size

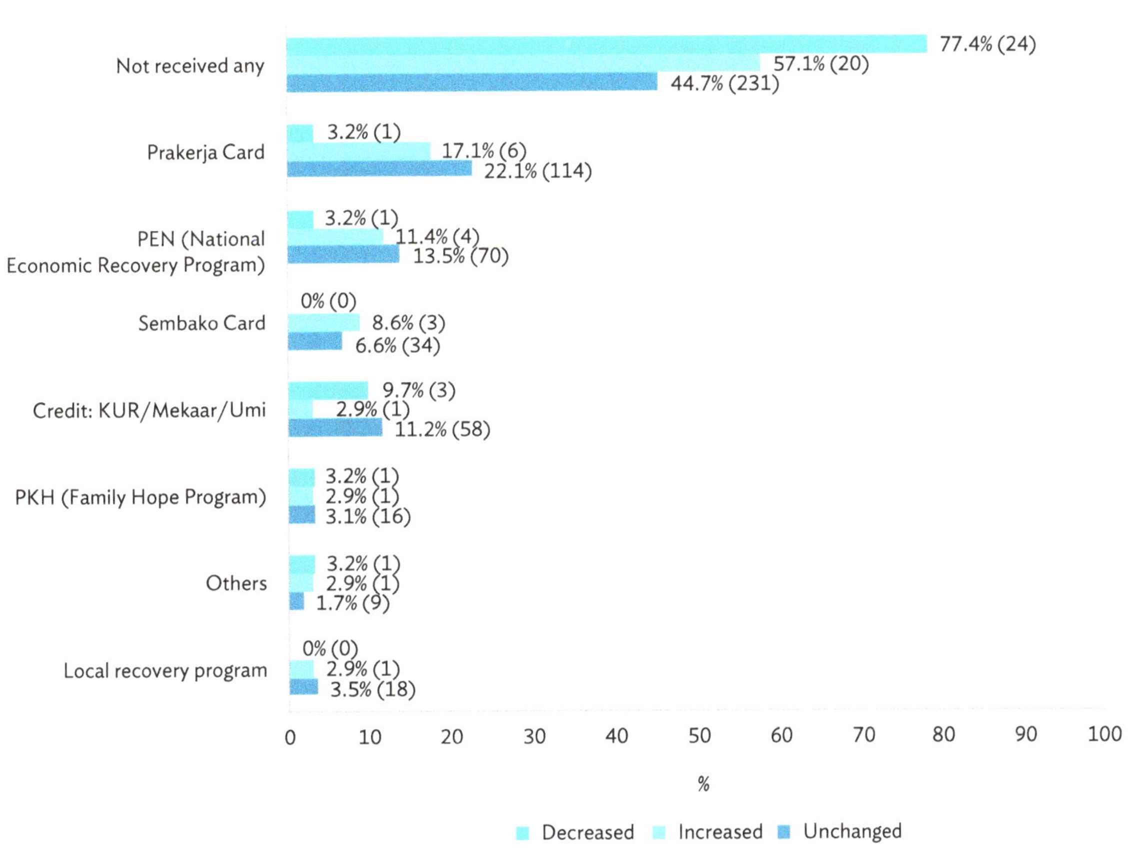

KUR = *Kredit Usaha Rakyat*, PEN = *Pemulihan Ekonomi Nasional*, PKH = *Program Keluarga Harapan*.
Notes: Support programs received by businesses between March 2020 (the beginning of the pandemic) to February 2021. Change in business size from March 2020 to March 2021. Business size refers to the size of business as of March 2021. Numbers in parentheses represent the total number of respondents for each category.
Source: Online survey of GoFood merchants.

recovery programs. This could partially be explained by well-operated MSMEs' relative proficiency in navigating application procedures, as noted by some of the survey respondents. Similarly, a likely reason for the observed relationship between receipt of government assistance and maintenance or increase of business size could be that these programs were effective in providing financial support to MSMEs.

H. The Performance of Women-Headed MSMEs during the Pandemic

The COVID-19 pandemic had a disproportionate socioeconomic impact on MSME business income, particularly for women and in developing countries such as Indonesia (UN Women 2020).

Globally, past economic downturns have often affected men more than women since men are more likely to be employed in industries that are closely tied to economic cycles, such as construction and manufacturing, while women are more likely to be employed in industries less susceptible to such cycles, such as health care and education. This has been shown to be the case especially in high-income countries (ILO 2020). However, the global contraction induced by the COVID-19 pandemic differed. The sectors most exposed to the curtailment of economic activity caused by lockdowns, including food services, comprise a sizable share of total female employment. Further, many women operate self-employed and micro businesses with relatively low levels of capitalization and are therefore more reliant on self-financing. This is especially true for women in the informal economy, which accounts for 60% of all employment in Indonesia. With a lack of access to credit and less capitalization, women were therefore more likely to close down their businesses for extended periods during the pandemic (OECD 2020).

Several findings from the Gojek surveys point to (i) differences in income losses between female-owned and male-owned businesses, (ii) divergent pandemic experiences for female versus male merchants in terms of domestic responsibilities, and (iii) different coping strategies and pandemic responses adopted by female and male merchants.

Figure 19 shows that the share of female-owned MSMEs in Indonesia experiencing a decline in revenue from offline and online sales during the pandemic (77.0%) was higher than the shares of both male-owned (72.8%) and jointly owned MSMEs (72.4%) experiencing a similar revenue reduction.[18] Disaggregating by type of sales, women-owned MSMEs witnessed declining offline and online sales

of 76.0% and 62.3%, respectively. This compares with declining offline and online sales of 74.6% and 60.1%, respectively, for male-owned MSMEs. What might have accounted for this discrepancy?

Figure 20, which utilizes responses to the phone survey to show merchants' difficulties in managing their households and businesses, reveals that there was a stark difference between female and male merchants when it came to managing household responsibilities during the pandemic. Women reported being more burdened by domestic work such as household chores, childcare, caregiving for elderly relatives, and overseeing their children's remote education—all while also managing a business.

Experiences of women GoFood merchants point to a "triple burden" during the pandemic—of business management, economic shock, and domestic responsibilities. This experience is encapsulated in the following quote from a woman entrepreneur:

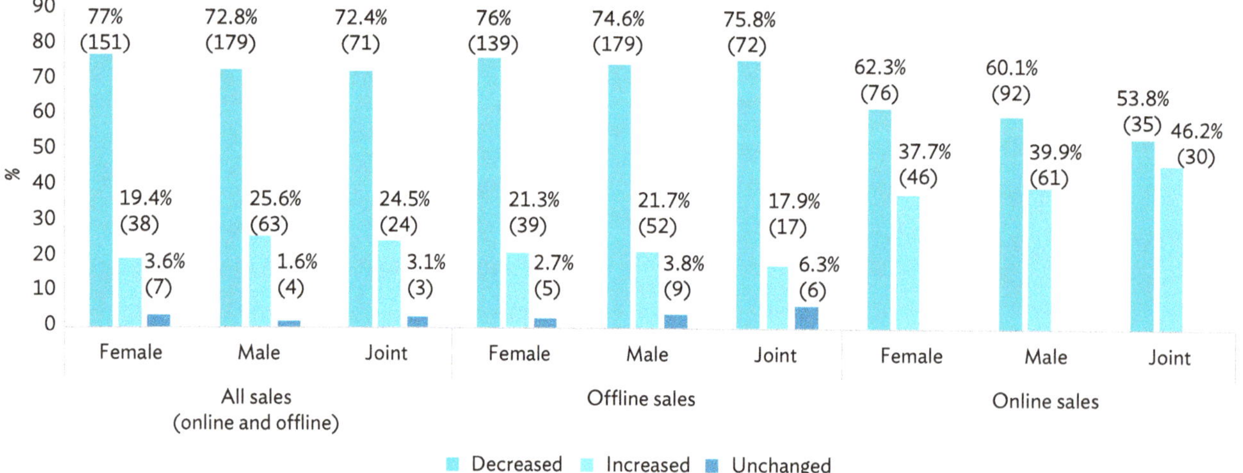

Figure 19: Change in Revenue during the Pandemic, by Merchant's Gender

Notes: Change in revenue from March 2020 to February 2021. The number of micro, small, and medium-sized enterprises that experienced changes in revenue by owner's gender varies for all sales (540), for offline sales (518),and for online sales (340). Numbers in parentheses represent the total number of respondents for each category. "Joint" refers to enterprises jointly owned by more than one (male or female) merchant.

Sources: Online survey of GoFood merchants and Gojek's administrative database.

---

[18]   Figure 19 was generated using merchant responses to Question Nos. 10, 11, and 20 in the online survey (see Appendix) and Gojek administrative database.

"I'm overwhelmed in the morning when I open up my store. At the same time I have to take care of my children, such as bathing them, feeding them, and my husband will go to work, so I'm overwhelmed... I have to take care of my kids and run my business at the same time. It's difficult to take care and manage customers' orders with that situation."

—Female respondent, 33 years old, Jabodetabek, self-employed, high school education or higher.

Figure 20: Managing Household and Business, by Merchant's Gender

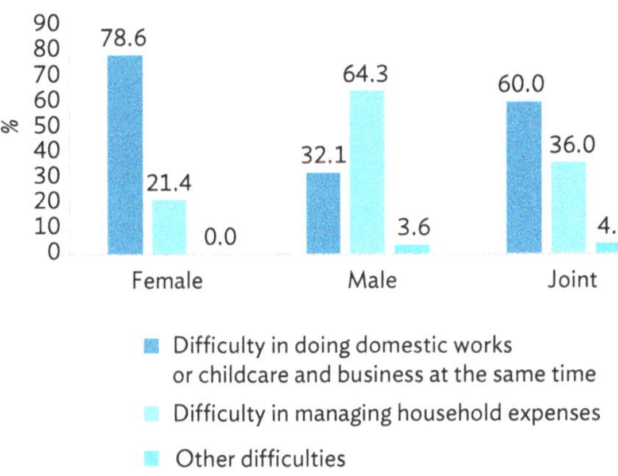

Note: Difficulties faced by GoFood merchants in managing household and business responsibilities and finances by gender of merchant. "Joint" refers to enterprises jointly owned by more than one (male or female) merchant.
Source: Phone survey of GoFood merchants.

The survey results have further highlighted variations in the socioeconomic impacts of the pandemic between women and men, particularly regarding domestic responsibilities and income losses. How then did women merchants manage to overcome this burden and keep their businesses afloat during the pandemic?

Figure 21 presents the coping strategies adopted by male and female merchants during the pandemic. Female merchants were more likely to spend less money on food, clothes, and leisure

than male merchants (64.1% vs. 53.6%) (Survey Question Nos. 12 and 20 in the Appendix). Male merchants were less likely to curtail spending on basic necessities to cope with the economic crisis triggered by the pandemic.

Figure 21: Coping Strategies during the Pandemic, by Merchant's Gender

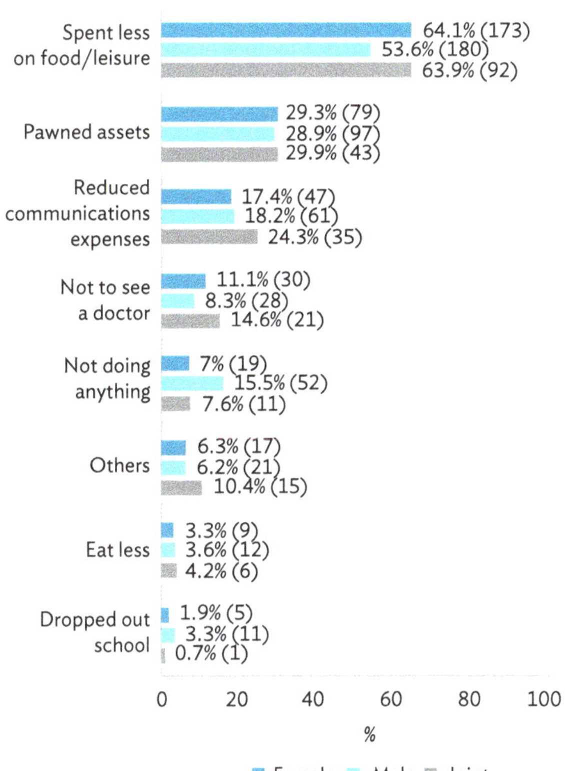

Notes: Coping strategies in the period between March 2020 (beginning of the pandemic) to February 2021. The numbers in parentheses represent the total number of respondents for each category. "Joint" refers to enterprises jointly owned by more than one (male or female) merchant.
Source: Online survey of GoFood merchants.

Further, the share of jointly owned enterprises that reported reducing their living expenses (63.9%) was remarkably close to that of female-owned enterprises. Considering the discrepancy in spending behavior between male and female merchants highlighted above, this suggests that women were more likely than men to handle decision-making related to expenditures in jointly owned enterprises during the pandemic.

Figure 22 presents sources of MSME financing during the pandemic by merchant's gender (Survey Question Nos. 13 and 20 in the Appendix). It paints a picture that aligns with pre-pandemic evidence, which suggests female-owned MSMEs are more likely to rely upon business income and only consider receiving loans from a financial institution when they need to fund business operations (Japhta et al. 2016). For example, female-owned GoFood MSMEs in Indonesia were more likely than male-owned MSMEs to rely upon savings (56.3% vs. 54.8%) and use business income (45.6% vs. 40.8%) for needed financing during the pandemic, while male merchants were more likely to take out a loan from a bank or a microfinance institution (23.5% vs. 21.5%).

Some women entrepreneurs explained their hesitation to borrow funds due to the potential risk of defaulting on the loan:

"My principle is that I don't want to take loans. So, it's just what I have. So, I just circulate my money. I do not dare to take loans. I am afraid that I can't pay it back."

—Female respondent, 40 years old, EJBN, self-employed, high school education or higher.

In spite of additional hardships and more widespread decreases in revenue, female-owned MSMEs ultimately outperformed their male-owned counterparts during the pandemic, as measured by average weekly sales and revenues.

Figure 22: Sources of Financing, by Merchant's Gender

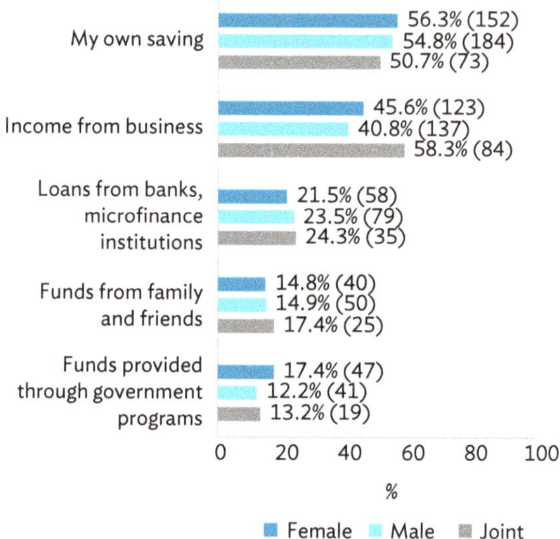

Notes: Sources of financing GoFood merchants used from March 2020 (beginning of the pandemic) to February 2021. The numbers in parentheses represent the total number of respondents for each category. "Joint" refers to enterprises jointly owned by more than one (male or female) merchant.

Source: Online survey of GoFood merchants.

V. Conclusion

In 2021–2022, Gojek and ADB undertook a joint study to assess the COVID-19 pandemic's impact on MSMEs that sell and market their food products on Gojek's GoFood platform, as well as the various coping strategies of merchants in response to the economic crisis. The objective was to gain a better understanding of the digitalization process among Indonesian MSMEs, while also exploring their resilience in the face of economic hardship. The survey's findings supported much of the literature on the adverse impacts of the COVID-19 pandemic,[19] particularly for self-employed and micro-sized enterprises, which are generally the most vulnerable during an economic crisis. Not surprisingly, those with low cash reserves were in the greatest peril of not surviving the pandemic. In addition, women merchants faced a unique "triple burden"—of business management, economic shock, and domestic responsibilities—that challenged them further as they strove to maintain a viable business amid a generational economic downturn.

Most merchants were reluctant to borrow needed funds from a financial institution for a variety of reasons ranging from fear of being unable to repay a loan to the religious prohibition against usury. Furthermore, insufficient beneficiary data hampered government assistance efforts during the pandemic, forcing some MSME owners to use their own savings, reduce spending on necessities, decrease the number of their employees, or even close their business. That is why the capacity to use online platforms and continue reaching their customer base throughout the pandemic was so critical for many MSMEs.

This report provides a range of evidence on Gojek's positive impact on MSMEs during the COVID-19 pandemic. A significant number of surveyed MSMEs noted they benefited from Gojek services, including the most vulnerable. As stated earlier, more than half of the GoFood merchants surveyed (51.5%) reported that using GoFood helped their business endure the economic crisis and another 41.8% credited Gojek for helping their business expand during the first year of the pandemic.

In addition to connecting merchants with customers, Gojek also continued to support businesses throughout the pandemic by offering business solutions that promote efficient operations (GoBiz), enable digital payments (GoPay), and offer financial services (GoModal). This study also revealed that, in facilitating the growth and resilience of MSMEs through their various digital business lines, platforms are also investing in their own success.

Platforms have supported MSMEs in many positive ways in Indonesia, and there is scope for further engagement and development. Several avenues in which online platforms can continue to grow their own business and support MSME merchants in the process are discussed below.

The surveys offered a unique opportunity for MSMEs to directly express their views about all aspects of their business relationship with Gojek. Pandemic conditions saw a multitude of MSMEs either join for the first time or try to expand their presence on online platforms. While offering the opportunity to reach new customers, this also led to increased competition for many merchants who may have already been struggling to remain profitable even before the pandemic. One way to further support MSMEs could be to consider assigning incumbent merchants and new entrants to the platform adequately broad service areas, rather than a fixed, distance-based perimeter.

---

[19]　See, for example, Shinozaki and Rao (2020).

Some participants in the phone survey expressed their desire for an improved user experience when conducting business through GoBiz. This feedback may have been due to the differing levels of digital and financial literacy among MSME owners. For instance, the online survey found that merchants with at least a high school education tended to use more than one online platform more frequently than merchants who do not. Given the higher capacity to adopt new technology and higher incidence of financial literacy among better educated merchants, there is an opportunity to expand inclusivity by identifying and aiding those who need additional assistance in navigating the functionalities of various online platforms. One example could be deepening the engagement with self-employed and micro-sized enterprises during the creation of their online banners, menus, and promotional advertisements.

Many merchants remain wary of taking out a loan from a financial institution for a variety of reasons. Gojek has responded to this reluctance with the introduction of its alternative financing solution, GoModal (Section IV). GoModal has also greatly simplified the disbursal and recovery of payments in comparison to a traditional bank loan. Such lending products can further increase the participation of some merchants, including women, who are less likely to engage in in-person meetings with loan officers. Notably, more female than male merchants used GoModal between March 2020 and March 2021, reflecting the program's success in providing financing to groups that are traditionally more hesitant to take a bank loan.

A common refrain in survey responses was merchant concerns over the fees associated with each delivery. This issue does not lend itself to an easy solution given the commercial priorities of online platforms and the fact that margins can be quite narrow in the food delivery sector. Reducing the minimum number of sales that self-employed and micro-sized enterprises must reach to receive reimbursement from the platform might be a way to improve cashflow management for more vulnerable merchants.

Another phone survey participant explained his wariness to participate in future promotional schemes after joining one that enabled his restaurant to reach a wider delivery area for a fee. He was charged Rp2,500 each time a potential customer clicked on his promotional advertisement, whether they ultimately placed an order through the GoFood app or not. While this merchant saw an increase in orders during the promotional period, including from outside his traditional delivery area, he ended up owing more in expenses due to numerous customer interactions with his promotion. In turn, another merchant commented that to avoid problems such as this, business owners needed to be very strategic when using promotions. He felt he had been successful because he managed his advertising budget wisely and did not join too many promotional schemes at the same time. These two examples suggest the potential for additional merchant education on how to utilize online promotions, with such courses and training tailored to different segments of MSMEs based on size, location, digital and financial literacy, among others.

MSMEs in peri-urban and remote areas can be at a disadvantage in delivering food to customers if additional delivery fees are required due to the distances involved in meal pickup and delivery, thereby making their products more expensive for customers. Some respondents to the phone survey also mentioned that the nonavailability of delivery riders in these areas hampered their online sales at times during the pandemic. This is a challenge that lacks an easy solution from online platforms alone and instead may require an innovative public-private collaborative approach.

Evaluating the government's MSME support program effectiveness is beyond the scope of this study. However, there is great potential for the government to facilitate development of the MSME sector in Indonesia, including through public-private collaborations. Based on the findings and observations from the survey, it can be inferred that accessibility to a range of government assistance programs available to MSME owners should be expanded. This can be accomplished through a combination of simplifying application processes and raising awareness through promotions that utilize a variety of media to reach different segments of the population. Other studies have found that Indonesian women were more likely than men to trust and use government services as a coping strategy during the pandemic.[20] There is thus an opportunity for the government to improve beneficiary targeting by improving program awareness and responding directly to beneficiary skepticism about the accessibly and effectiveness of such assistance programs.

A regularly updated MSME database that is integrated across government institutions can also help enhance the targeting and distribution of needed assistance. While there may be administrative and technical hurdles to creating such a database, its potential value to MSME merchants is evident in the survey responses of many participants, who expressed their unfamiliarity with the application procedures and other requirements for key government assistance programs. Further, an opportunity exists to leverage the comparative advantage of online platforms which have real-time access to a wealth of transactions and financial data from hundreds of thousands of merchant–partners.

The increasing visibility of food delivery riders during the pandemic focused public attention on their welfare. Some have even urged the issuance of government guidelines in all Southeast Asian markets—derived through dialogue among regulators, online platforms, and rider representatives—to provide both clarity and flexibility in the treatment of workers who are key to the continued success and growth of the region's food delivery industry.[21]

In conclusion, this study shows that Gojek has enabled MSMEs to enhance their visibility to potential consumers in spite of mobility restrictions and to reach a wider customer base than otherwise would have been possible during the pandemic. For some, this meant survival amid an extremely challenging economic environment. For others, Gojek helped facilitate the growth of their business by channeling new customers directly to them. The encouraging findings related to MSME resilience during the economic turmoil of the pandemic point to the benefits of digitalization in general. To facilitate an inclusive recovery and better equip MSMEs to deal with the next crisis, it is important to adequately prepare the MSME sector for a more digital future. This study contributes to the evidence-based that can inform future policy decisions and industry practices—to better support MSMEs, accelerate the process of recovery from the pandemic's most severe economic impacts, and pave the way for inclusive growth.

---

[20]   See, for example, Elhan-Kayalar et al. (2022).

[21]   See, for example, Momentum Works (2021, 2022).

Appendix: Survey Questionnaire*

Q1: **What is your role or position in this business?**
   A. Owner
   B. Manager
   C. Other Staff

Figure A.1: Merchant's Position in the Business

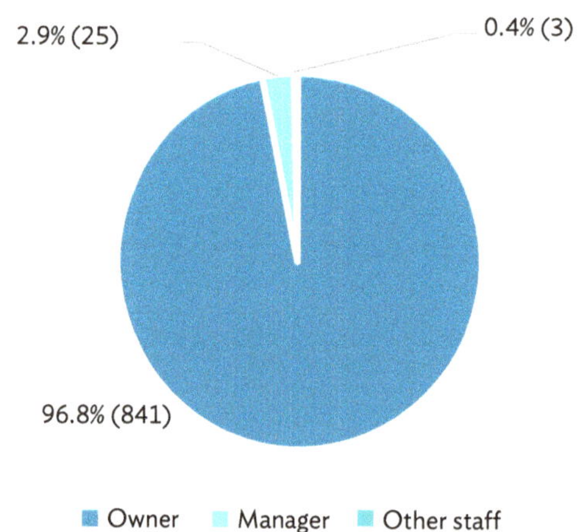

Note: Numbers in parentheses represent the total number of respondents for each category.
Source: Online survey of GoFood merchants.

Figure A.2: Merchant's Position in the Business, by Gender

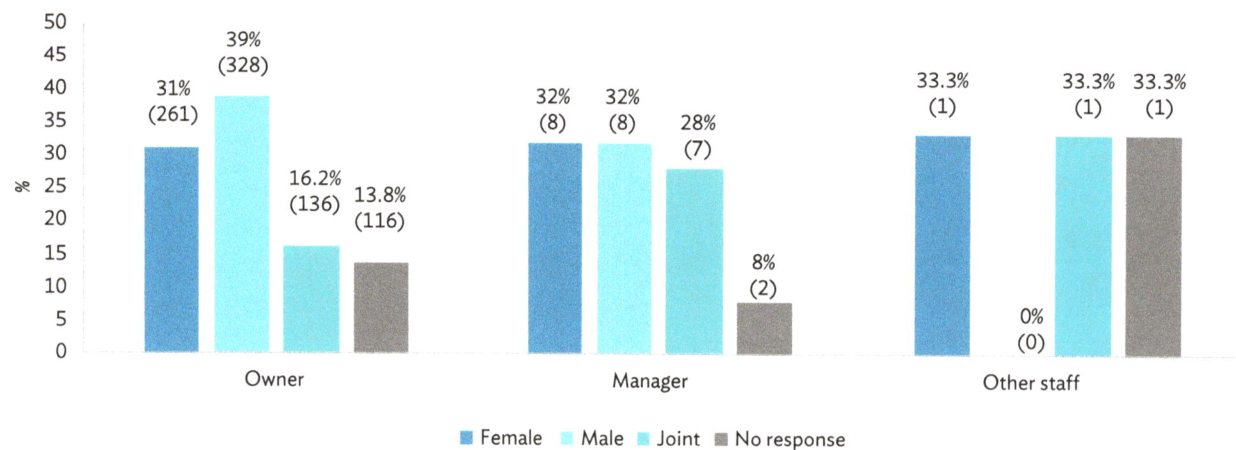

Note: Numbers in parentheses represent the total number of respondents for each category.
         "Joint" refers to enterprises jointly owned by more than one (male or female) merchant.
Source: Online survey of GoFood merchants.

---

*   In this section, "Q(number)" denotes "online survey question(number)."

Q2:   What is your decision-making role in your business?

A. I am the main decision maker for this business

B. I am involved in business decision making, together with someone else

C. I am not involved in the business decision making, someone else is

Figure A.3: Merchant's Decision-Making Role in the Business

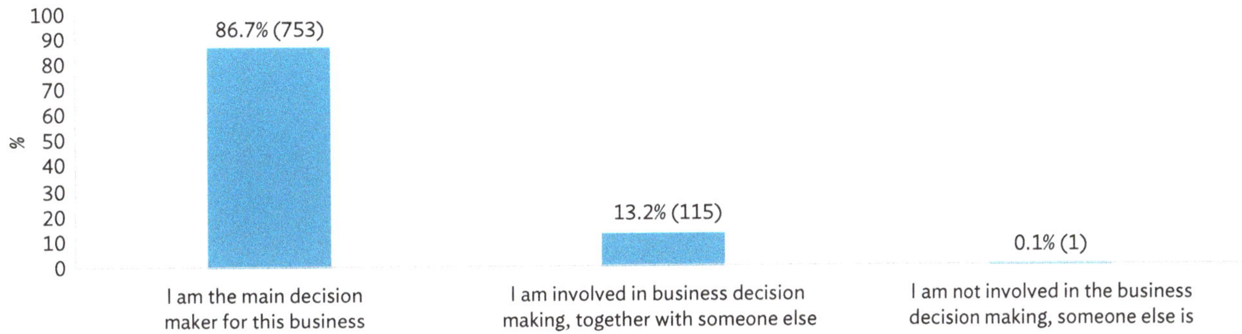

Note: Numbers in parentheses represent the total number of respondents for each category.

Source: Online survey of GoFood merchants.

Figure A.4: Merchant's Decision-Making Role in the Business, by Gender

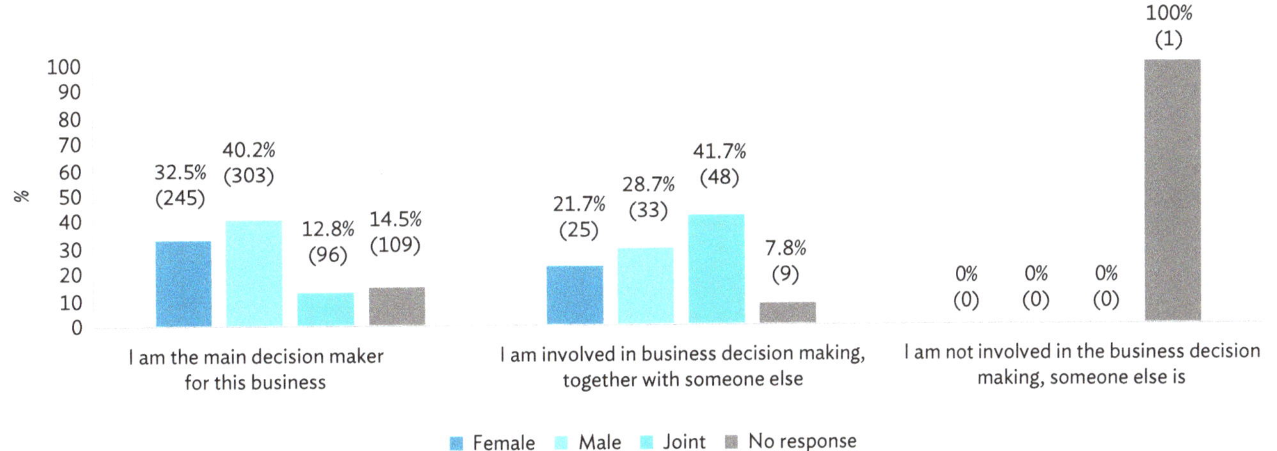

Note: Numbers in parentheses represent the total number of respondents for each category.
         "Joint" refers to enterprises jointly owned by more than one (male or female) merchant.

Source: Online survey of GoFood merchants.

Q3:   What is your involvement in daily business management and administration?

A. I am involved in the daily business management and administration

B. I am involved in the business management and administration most of the times, but not every day

C. I am not involved in the business management and administration

Figure A.5: Merchant's Involvement in Daily Business Management and Administration

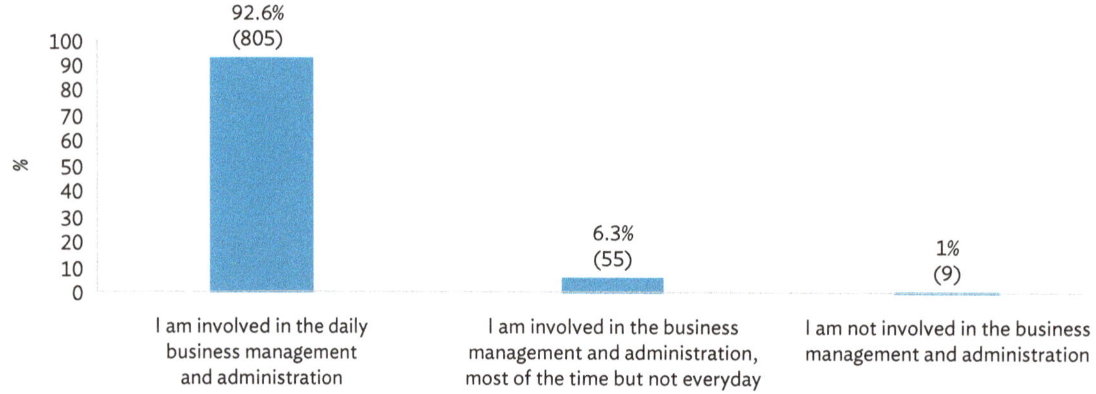

Note: Numbers in parentheses represent the total number of respondents for each category.
Source: Online survey of GoFood merchants.

Figure A.6: Merchant's Involvement in Daily Business Management and Administration, by Gender

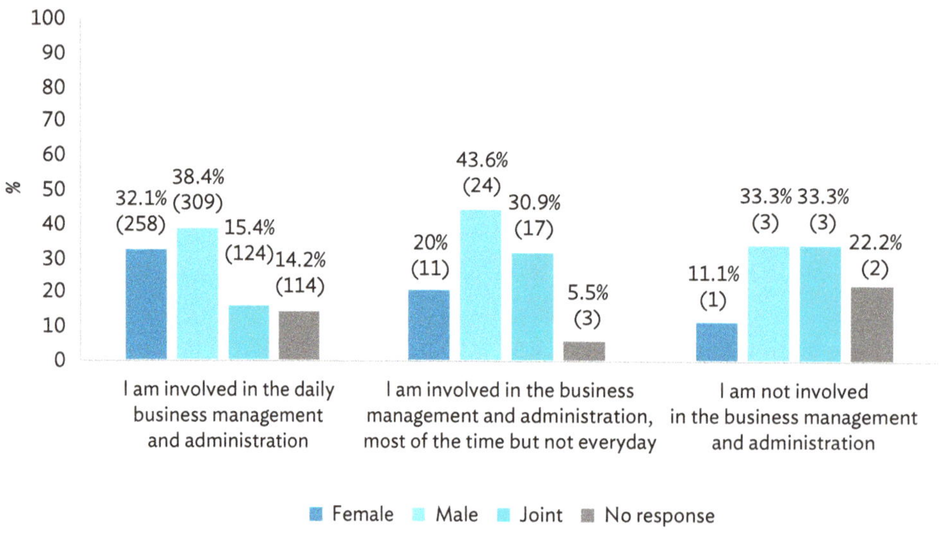

Note: Numbers in parentheses represent the total number of respondents for each category.
         "Joint" refers to enterprises jointly owned by more than one (male or female) merchant.
Source: Online survey of GoFood merchants.

Q4:   Is this business:
A. My primary source of income
B. My secondary or additional source of income

Figure A.7: Business as Source of Income

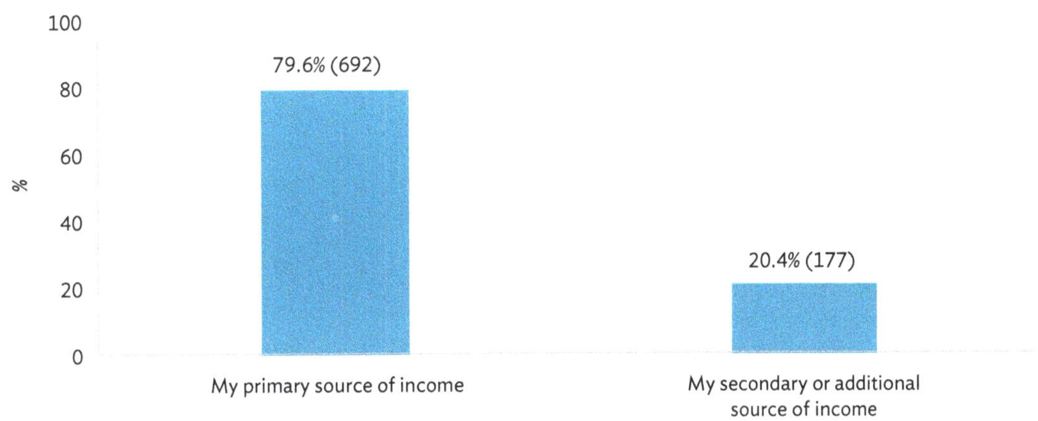

Note: The numbers in parentheses represent the total number of respondents for each category.
Source: Online survey of GoFood merchants.

Figure A.8: Business as Source of Income, by Business Size

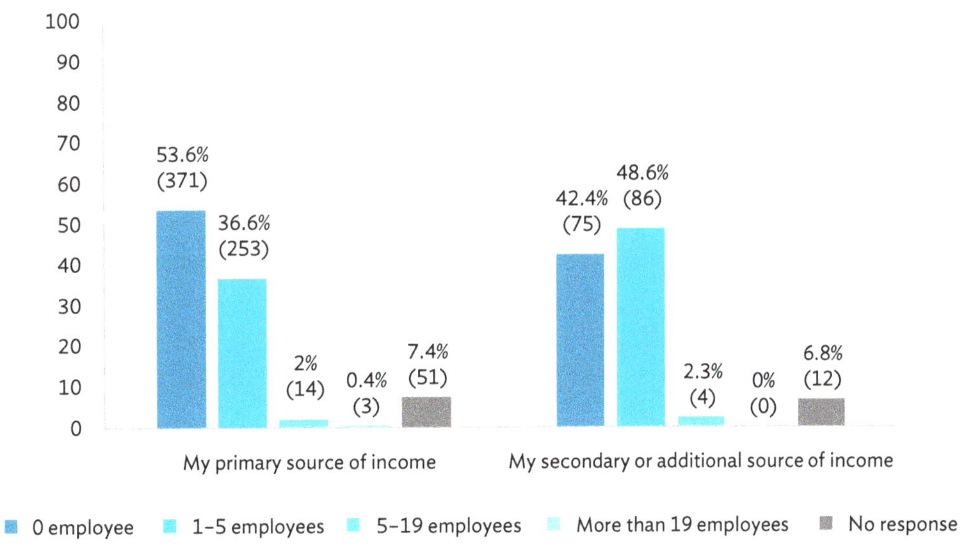

Note: Numbers in parentheses represent the total number of respondents for each category.
Source: Online survey of GoFood merchants.

Q5:   When was this business established?

Figure A.9: Establishment Year of Business

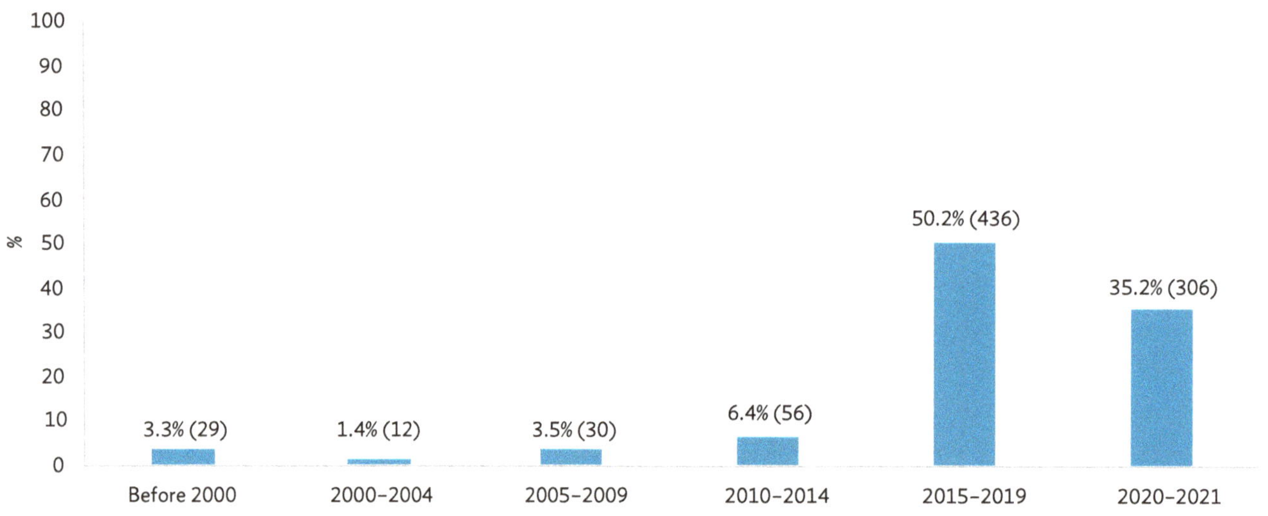

Note: Numbers in parentheses represent the total number of respondents for each category.
Source: Online survey of GoFood merchants.

Q6:   In question 6, merchants were asked in which district (kecamatan) their business is located. For brevity, merchants' responses to question 6 are not included here.

Q7:   In March 2021, how many employees are/were involved in this business (including yourself)?
   A.   I work by myself, no other employees
   B.   Between 1 and 4 employees
   C.   Between 5 and 19 employees
   D.   More than 19 employees

Figure A.10: Business Size by Number of Employees, March 2021

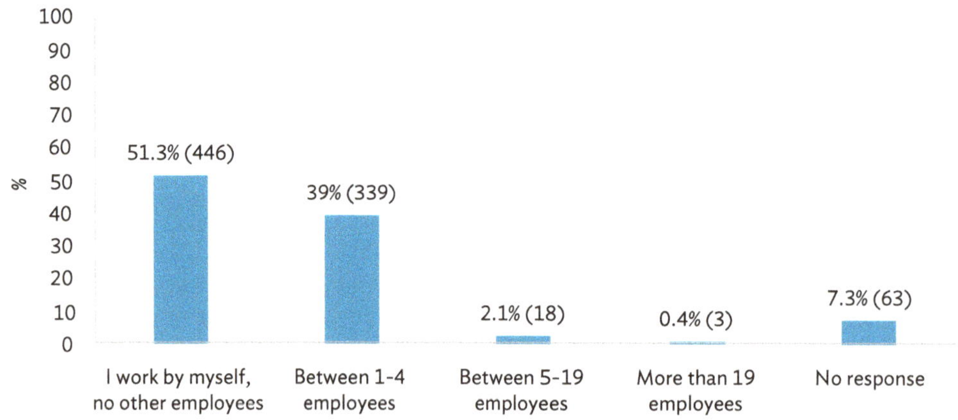

Note: Numbers in parentheses represent the total number of respondents for each category.
Source: Online survey of GoFood merchants.

Q8:   In March 2020, how many employees are/were involved in this business (including yourself)?

    A. I work by myself, no other employees

    B. Between 1 and 4 employees

    C. Between 5 and 19 employees

    D. More than 19 employees

Figure A.11: Business Size by Number of Employees, March 2020

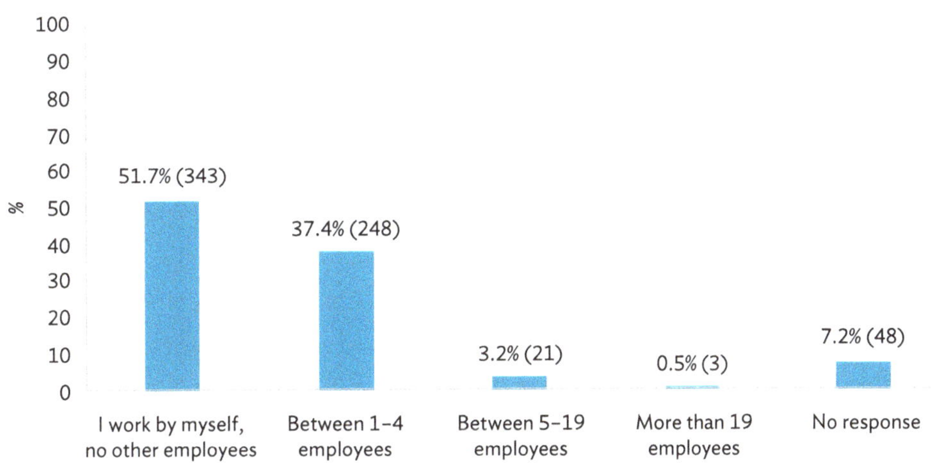

Note: Numbers in parentheses represent the total number of respondents for each category.

Source: Online survey of GoFood merchants.

Q9:   In March 2019, how many employees are/were involved in this business (including yourself)?

    A. I work by myself, no other employees

    B. Between 1 and 4 employees

    C. Between 5 and 19 employees

    D. More than 19 employees

    E. My business was established in 2020

Figure A.12: Business Size by Number of Employees, March 2019

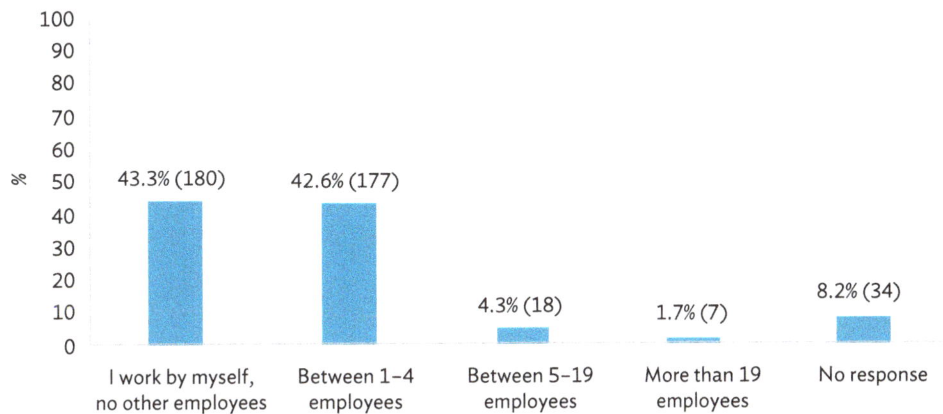

Notes: Includes only those businesses operational as of March 2019. Numbers in parentheses represent the total number of respondents for each category.

Source: Online survey of GoFood merchants.

Q10: **Since COVID-19 (beginning of March 2020) until end of February 2021, overall (online and offline) revenue from the business:**
A.   Increased Less than 10%
B.   Increased 11–30%
C.   Increased 31–50%
D.   Increased more than 50%
E.   Decreased Less than 10%
F.   Decreased 11–30%
G.   Decreased 31–50%
H.   Decreased more than 50%
I.   Unchanged

Figure A.13: Change in Businesses' Overall Revenue from Online and Offline Sales

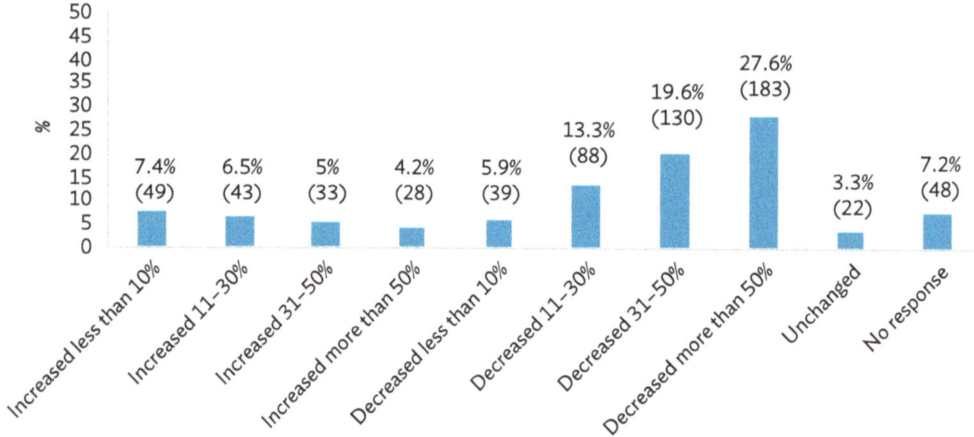

Notes: Includes only those businesses operational as of March 2020. Numbers in parentheses represent the total number of respondents for each category.
Source: Online survey of GoFood merchants.

Q11: **Since COVID-19 (beginning of March 2020) until end of February 2021, offline (at restaurant or food stall) revenue from the business:**
A.   Increased Less than 10 %
B.   Increased 11–30%
C.   Increased 31–50%
D.   Increased more than 50%
E.   Decreased Less than 10 %
F.   Decreased 11–30%
G.   Decreased 31–50%
H.   Decreased more than 50%
I.   Unchanged
J.   My store only sells online

Figure A.14: Change in Businesses' Revenue from Offline Sales

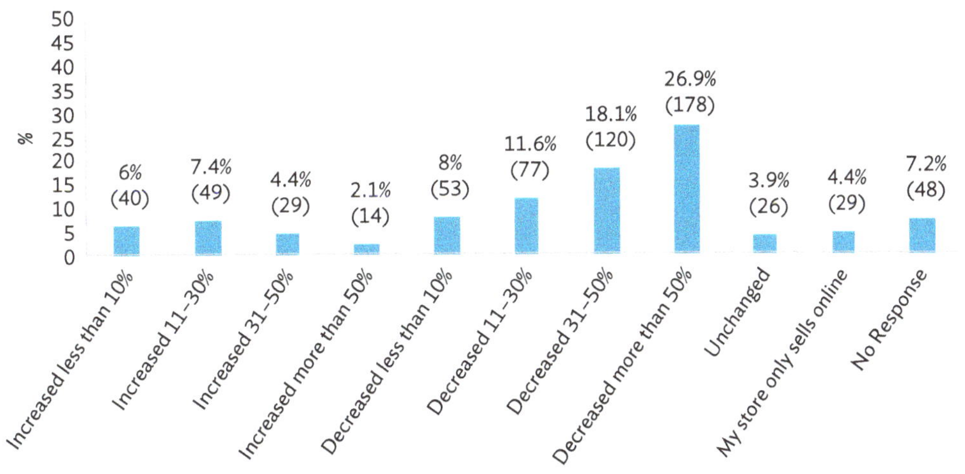

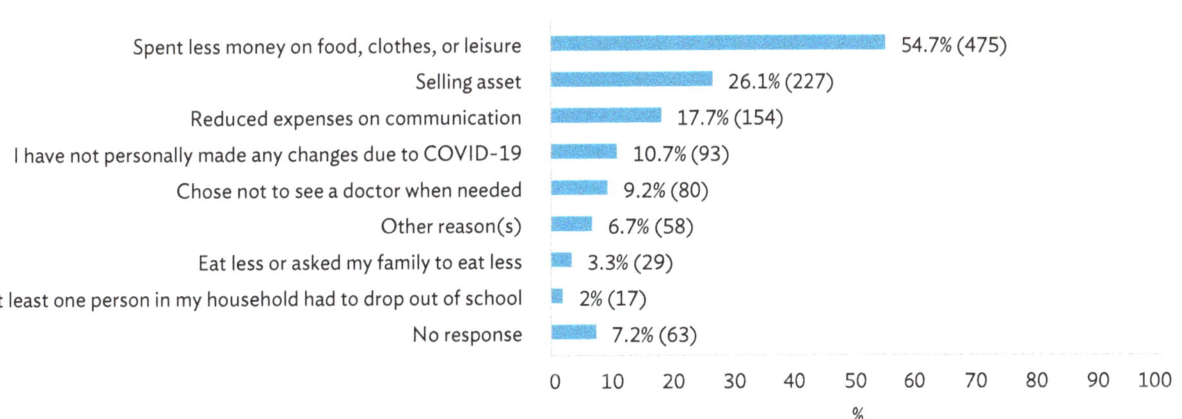

Notes: Includes only those businesses operational as of March 2021. Numbers in parentheses represent the total number of respondents for each category.

Source: Online survey of GoFood merchants.

Q12:   **Since COVID-19 (beginning of March 2020) until the end of February 2021, have you personally made any of the following changes to help cope with the situation? (Multiple answers are allowed)**

A.   Spent less money on food, clothes, or leisure

B.   Eat less or asked my family to eat less

C.   At least one person in my household had to drop out of school due to financial constraints

D.   Reduced expenses on communication (e.g. phone, internet, etc.)

E.   Chose not to see a doctor when needed

F.   Other reason(s), please specify ____

G.   I have not personally made any changes due to COVID-19

Figure A.15: Merchant's Coping Strategies

COVID-19 = coronavirus disease.

Note: Numbers in parentheses represent the total number of respondents for each category.

Source: Online survey of GoFood merchants.

Q13:   I have availed of the following financing sources during March 2020–February 2021 period:
    A.   My own savings
    B.   Funds from family and friends
    C.   Loans from banks, microfinance institutions
    D.   Funds provided through government programs
    E.   Income from business

Figure A.16: Business Financing Source

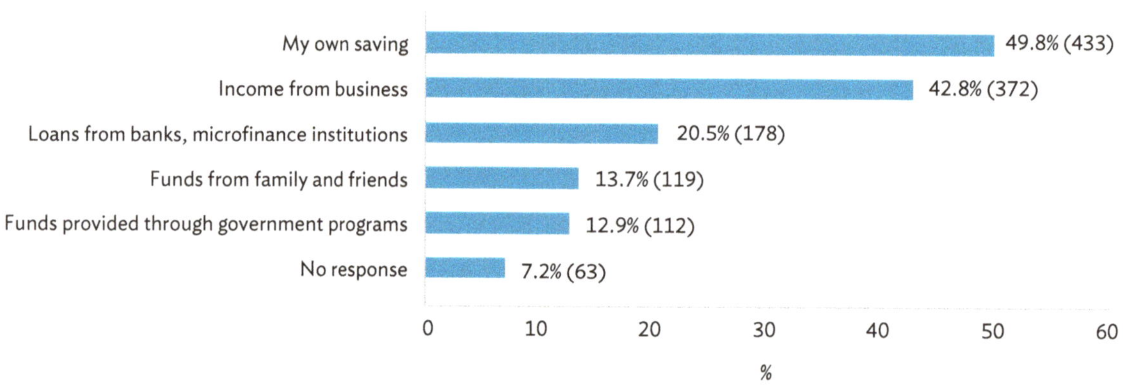

Note: Numbers in parentheses represent the total number of respondents for each category.
Source: Online survey of GoFood merchants.

Q14:   Which of the following government programs have you received during the pandemic (after 1 March 2020 until the end of February 2021)? (Multiple answers are allowed)
    A.   Credit: KUR/Mekaar/Umi
    B.   PEN (the National Economic Recovery Program)
    C.   Local recovery program
    D.   PKH (Program Keluarga Harapan)
    E.   Sembako Card
    F.   Prakerja
    G.   Other program(s): _______________________________
    H.   I do not receive support from any government program

Figure A.17: Government Support Received by Merchants During the Pandemic

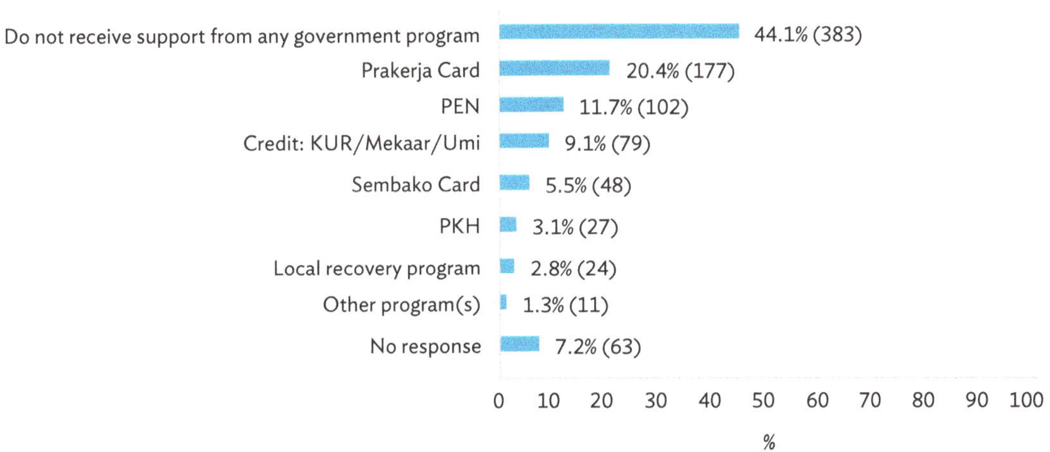

KUR = *Kredit Usaha Rakyat*, PEN = *Pemulihan Ekonomi Nasional*, PKH = *Program Keluarga Harapan*.
Note: Numbers in parentheses represent the total number of respondents for each category.
Source: Online survey of GoFood merchants.

Q15:   How long have you been using apps within the Gojek ecosystem (e.g. GoBiz, GoFood, GoPay, GoSend, MokaPOS, etc) to run/help this business?

A. I only started using them since the spread of COVID-19
B. Less than one year but did not start because of COVID-19
C. Between 1 and 3 years
D. More than 3 years

Figure A.18: Length of Time Merchants Used Gojek Applications

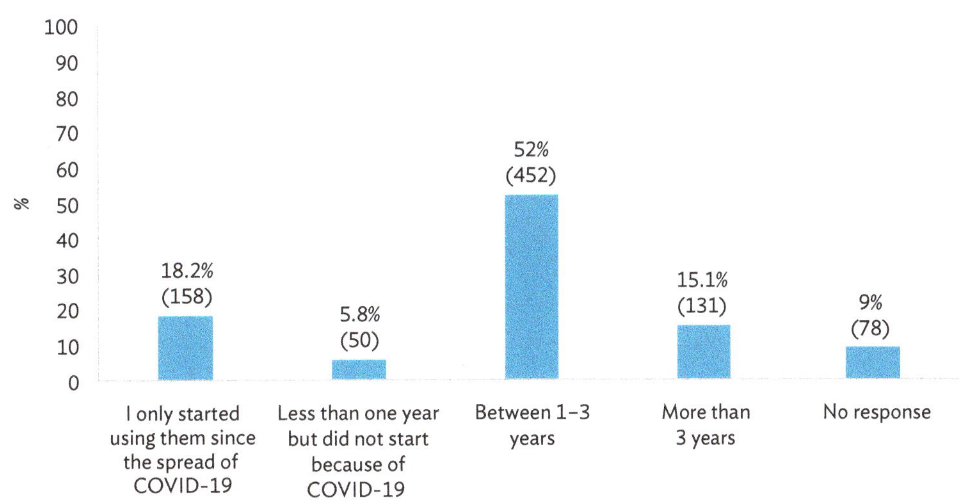

COVID-19 = coronavirus disease.
Notes: This figure is generated using the date of the merchant's first transaction on GoFood platform and merchant's survey responses. Numbers in parentheses represent the total number of respondents for each category.
Source: Online survey of GoFood merchants and Gojek's administrative database.

Q16: **How long have you been using other online marketplaces (e.g. Facebook, Instagram, WhatsApp, Website, Tokopedia, Shopee, etc.)?**

a. I only started using them since the spread of COVID-19

b. Less than one year, but did not start because of COVID-19

c. Between 1 and 3 years

d. More than 3 years

e. I do not use other online marketplaces

Figure A.19: Length of Time Merchants Used Other Online Marketplaces

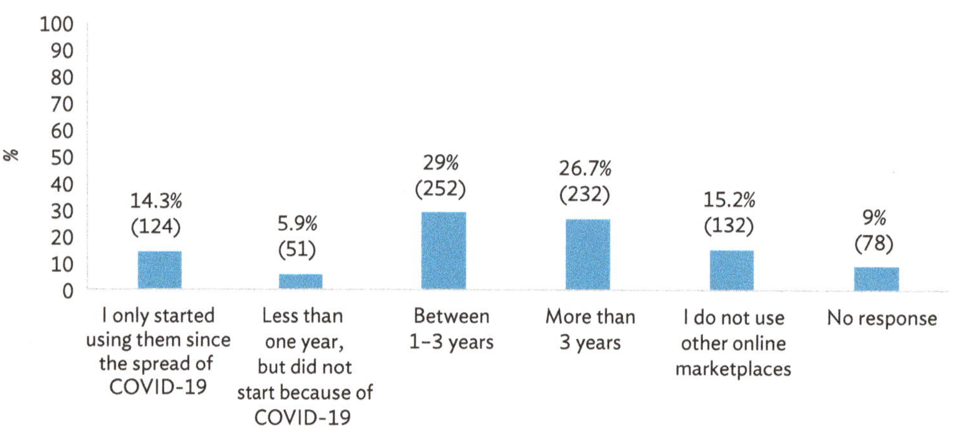

COVID-19 = coronavirus disease.
Note: Numbers in parentheses represent the total number of respondents for each category.
Source: Online survey of GoFood merchants.

Q17: **Can you specify which of the following Gojek products you have used since the spread of the COVID-19 pandemic (between March 2020 to February 2021)? (Multiple answers are allowed)**

A. GoBiz

B. GoFood

C. GoPay (to accept payment in store)

D. GoPay (to accept payment online

E. GoSend

F. GoModal

G. GoFresh

H. MokaPOS

I. GoStore

J. Selly Keyboard

Figure A.20: Gojek Products used by Merchants since COVID-19 Pandemic

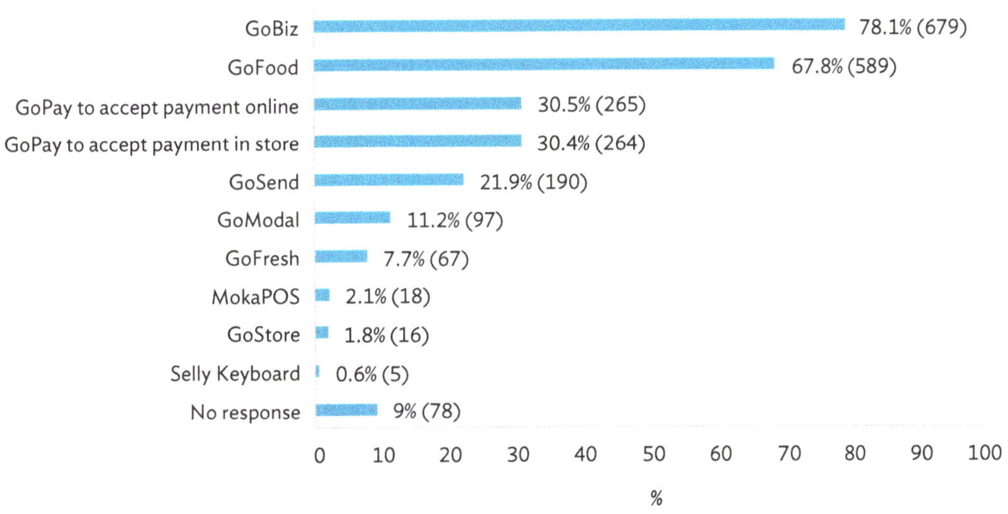

COVID-19 = coronavirus disease.
Note: Numbers in parentheses represent the total number of respondents for each category.
Source: Online survey of GoFood merchants.

Q18:   Since COVID-19 (March 2020 until the end of February 2021), how has using the apps from Gojek affected your business?

A.   Gojek has helped my business expand

B.   Gojek has helped my business survive

C.   Gojek has not helped my business

D.   I am unsure whether it made a difference for my business

Figure A.21: Role of Gojek during the Pandemic

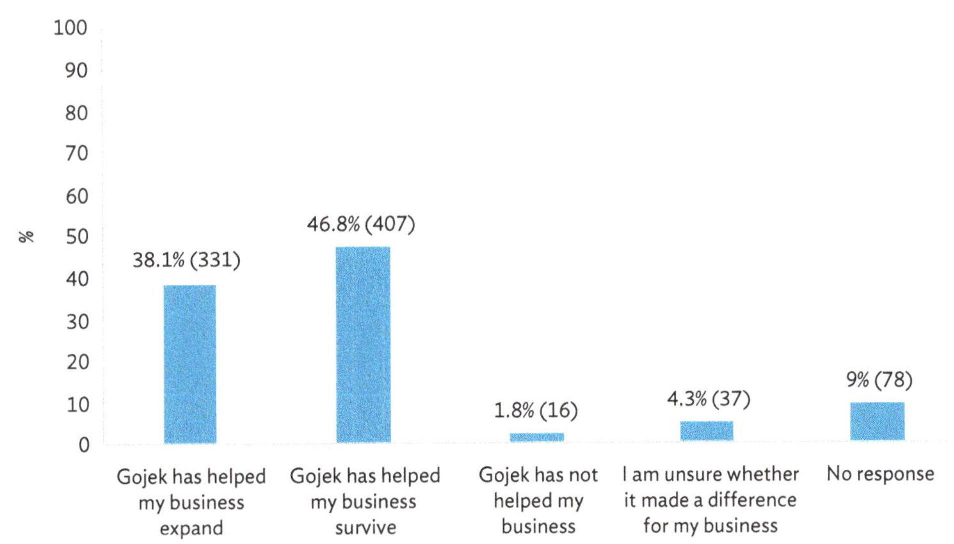

Note: Numbers in parentheses represent the total number of respondents for each category.
Source: Online survey of GoFood merchants.

Q19: **How much do you agree with the following statement: Using Gojek apps (e.g., GoBiz) for business allows me to take care of domestic and family responsibilities (e.g., I have time to spend with my family or to do some childcare responsibilities)**

A. Strongly agree
B. Agree
C. Neutral
D. Disagree
E. Strongly disagree

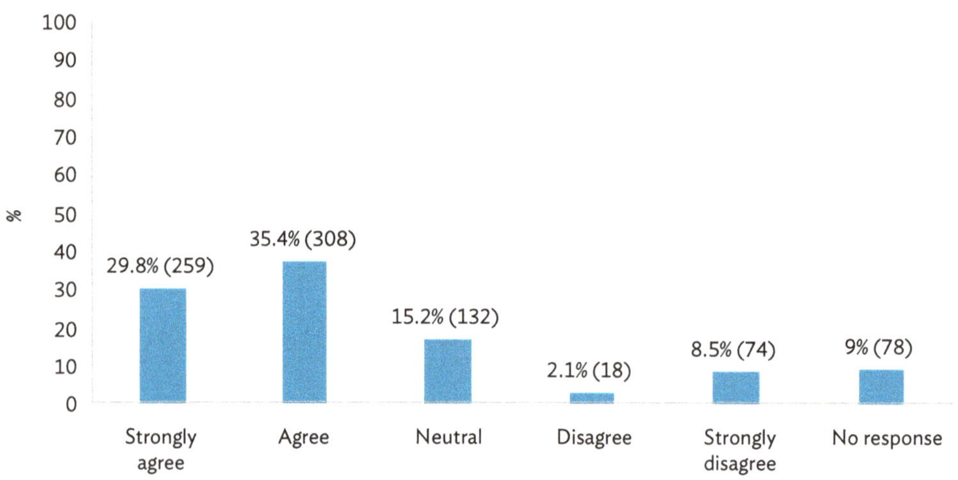

Figure A.22: GoFood Merchant's Domestic and Family Responsibilities

Note: Numbers in parentheses represent the total number of respondents for each category.
Source: Online survey of GoFood merchants.

Figure A.23: GoFood Merchant's Domestic and Family Responsibilities, by Gender

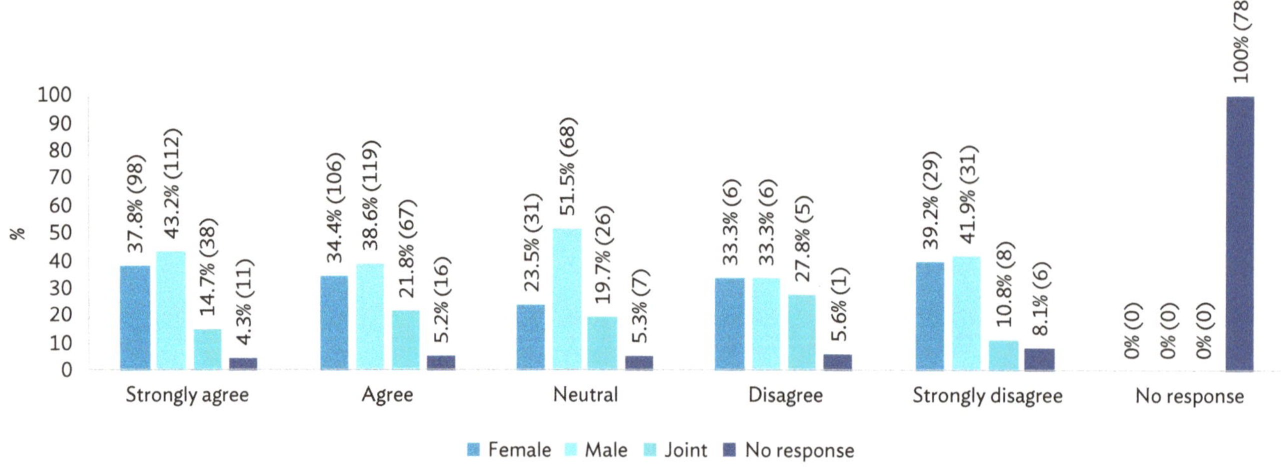

Note: Numbers in parentheses represent the total number of respondents for each category.
          "Joint" refers to enterprises jointly owned by more than one (male or female) merchant.
Source: Online survey of GoFood merchants.

Q20: **What is your gender?**
- A. Female
- B. Male
- C. I'd rather not answer

Figure A.24: Merchant's Gender

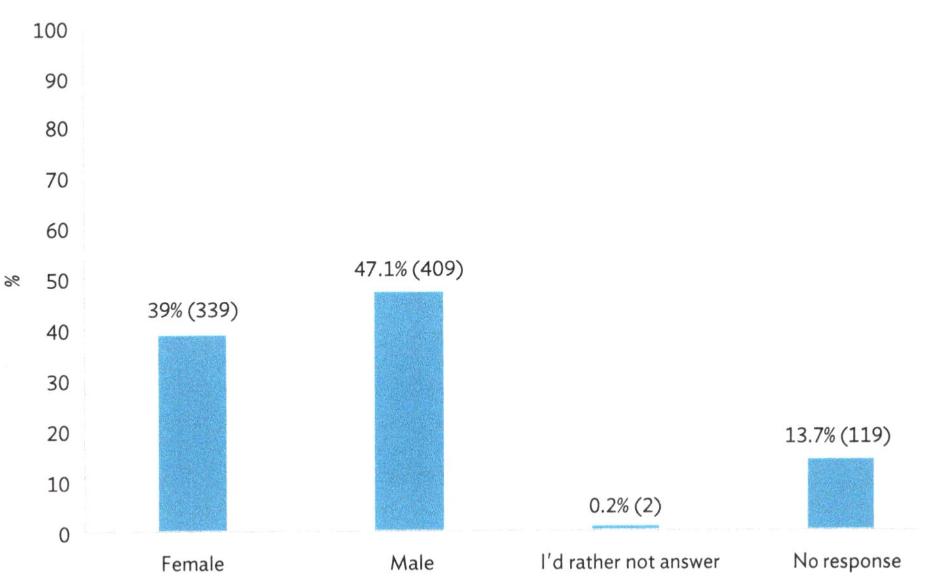

Note: Numbers in parentheses represent the total number of respondents for each category.
Source: Online survey of GoFood merchants.

Q21: What is your age in years?

Figure A.25: Merchant's Age

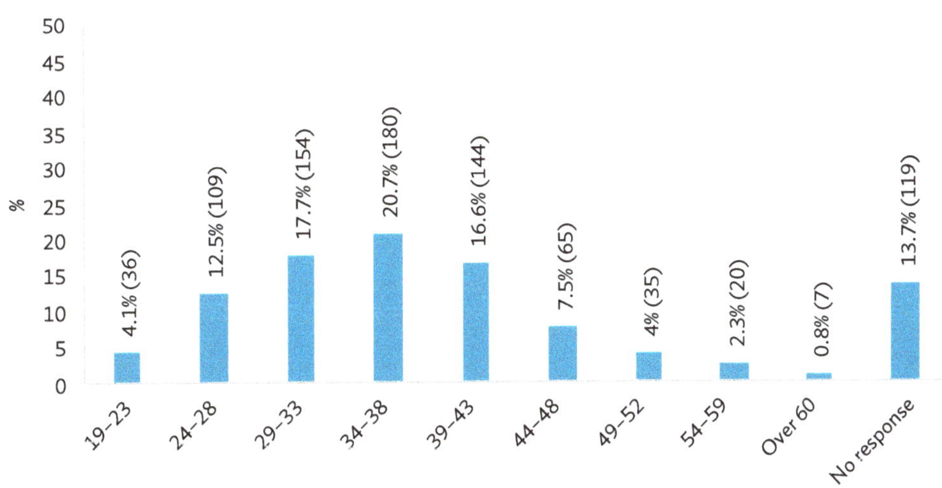

Note: Numbers in parentheses represent the total number of respondents for each category.
Source: Online survey of GoFood merchants.

Q22: What is your highest educational attainment?

A. Did not complete primary school
B. Elementary School
C. Junior High School
D. Senior High School
E. Vocational
F. Diploma I/II/III
G. Diploma IV/Bachelor
H. Master/Doctoral
I. No formal education

Figure A.26: Merchant's Level of Education

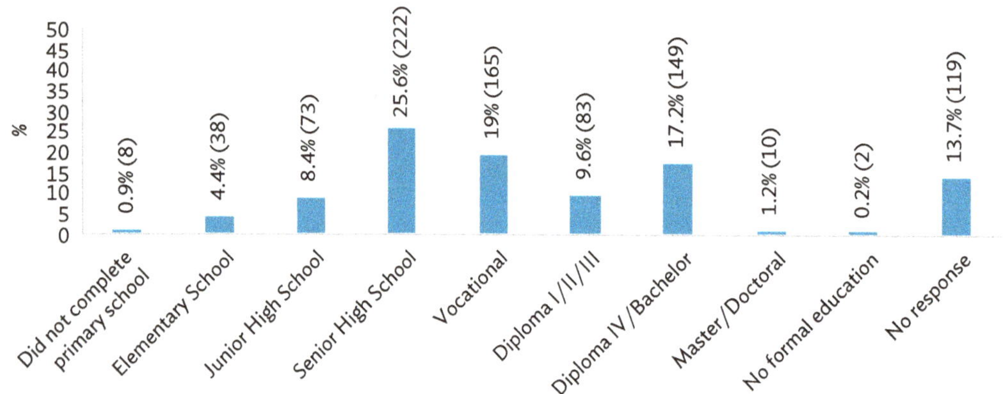

Note: Numbers in parentheses represent the total number of respondents for each category.
Source: Online survey of GoFood merchants.

Q23: The business owner is:

A. A woman
B. A man
C. Joint owner (all women)
D. Joint owner (all men)
E. Joint owner (women and men)

Figure A.27: GoFood Business Owner's Gender

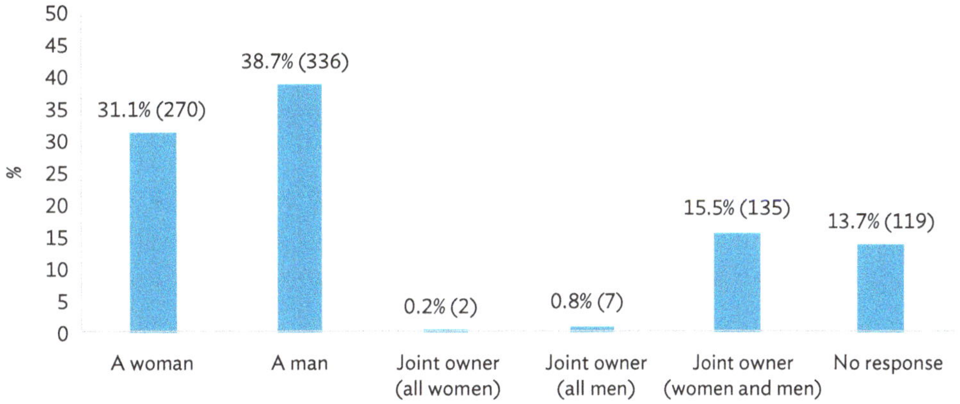

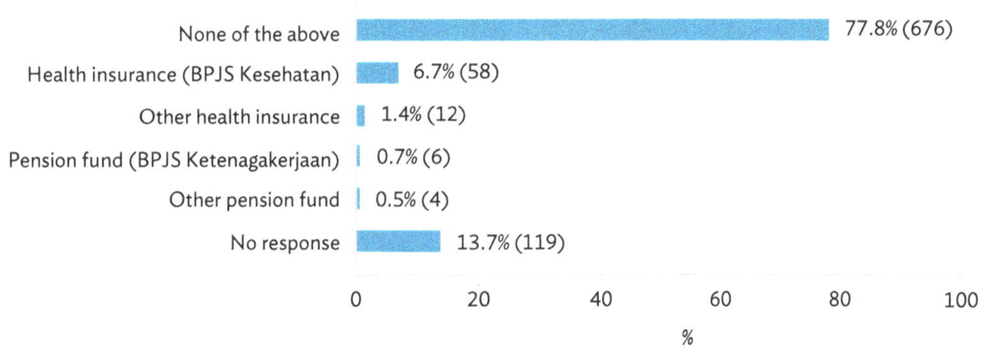

Notes: Numbers in parentheses represent the total number of respondents for each category.
         "Joint" refers to enterprises jointly owned by more than one (male or female) merchant.
Source: Online survey of GoFood merchants.

Q24: Does this business provide pension funds and health insurance for the employees? (Multiple answers are allowed)

A. Health insurance (BPJS Kesehatan)
B. Pension fund (BPJS Ketenagakerjaan)
C. Other health insurance
D. Other pension fund
E. None of the above

Figure A.28: Provision of Insurance and Pension Fund by Businesses for Employees

BPJS Kesehatan = *Badan Penyelenggara Jaminan Sosial Kesehatan* (Healthcare and Social Security Administration),
BPJS Ketenagakerjaan= *Badan Penyelenggara Jaminan Sosial Ketenagakerjaan* (Social Security and Employment Agency).
Note: Numbers in parentheses represent the total number of respondents for each category.
Source: Online survey of GoFood merchants.

Q25–Q28: Questions 25–26 asked merchants whether they provide any other health insurance or pension funds to their employees. Question 27 asked merchant's GoPay details to credit tokens for their participation in the online survey. Question 28 asked whether the merchants would participate in a follow-up phone survey, and for their contact details if they would like to do so. Responses to questions 25–28 are open-ended and are not included here.

References

ADB. 2022. *Asian Development Outlook: Mobilizing Taxes for Development*. Manila: Asian Development Bank.

Al Jazeera. 2021. COVID Slammed Indonesia's Economy Hard in 2020, Data Shows. February 4.

Amelia, L., D. S. Nurshadrina, V. T. Indrio, W. Larasati, and A. Suryahadi. 2022. The Impact of the COVID-19 Pandemic on MSMEs and the Role of Digitalization on Businesses' Resilience in Indonesia. *Technical Report*. Manila: Asian Development Bank.

Anatan, L. and Nur. 2023. Micro, Small, and Medium Enterprises' Readiness for Digital Transformation in Indonesia. *Economies*. 11 (6). pp. 156–177.

Asiati, D., N. Ngadi, Y. N. Aini, and Y. A. Purba. 2021. Sustainability of MSMEs in Indonesia: Learnings From COVID-19 Impact. In N. Baporikar, ed., *Handbook of Research on Sustaining SMEs and Entrepreneurial Innovation in the Post-COVID-19 Era*. Hershey, PA: IGI Global.

Baihaqqy, M. R. I., Disman, Nugraha, and M. Sari. 2020. The Correlation Between Education Level and Understanding of Financial Literacy and its Effect on Investment Decisions in Capital Markets. *Journal of Education and E-learning Research*. 7 (3). pp. 306-313.

Bank Indonesia. 2022. Digitalisation Increasing Economic Productivity. *News Release*. February 2.

Bartik, A. W., M. Bertrand, Z. B. Cullen, E. L. Glaeser, M. Luca, and C. T. Stanton. 2020. How Are Small Businesses Adjusting to COVID-19? Early Evidence from a Survey. *NBER Working Paper* 26989. Cambridge, MA: National Bureau of Economic Research.

DKI Jakarta Provincial Government. 2021. What is Social Cash Transfer Program (BST)? https://corona.jakarta.go.id/en/informasi-bantuan-sosial.

Eggers, F. 2020. Masters of Disasters? Challenges and Opportunities for SMEs in Times of Crisis. *Journal of Business Research*. 116. pp. 199–208.

Elhan-Kayalar, Y., Y. Sawada, and Y. van der Muelen Rodgers. 2022. Gender, Entrepreneurship, and Coping with the COVID-19 Pandemic. *Asia and the Pacific Policy Studies*. 9 (3). pp. 222–245.

Eloksari, E. A. 2020. Ministry, e-Commerce Team Up to Hold Online Classes for SMEs. *The Jakarta Post*. October 5.

Google, Temasek, and Bain & Company. 2022. e-Conomy SEA 2022 Report. https://economysea.withgoogle.com/report/.

Investment Coordinating Board. 2021. *Kolaborasi antara Kementerian Investasi dengan Gojek Memberdayakan UMKM* (The collaboration between the Ministry of Investment and GoJek Empowers MSMEs).

ILO. 2020. The COVID-19 Response: Getting Gender Equality Right for a Better Future for Women at Work. *Policy Brief*. Geneva: International Labour Organization.

Japhta, R., P. Murthy, Y. Fahmi, A. Marina, and A. Gupta. 2016. *Women-owned SMEs in Indonesia: A Golden Opportunity for Local Financial Institutions*. International Finance Corporation and USAID.

Kartono, R., and J. K. Tjahjadi. 2021. Factors Affecting Consumers' Intentions to Use Online Food Delivery Services during the COVID-19 Outbreak in the Jabodetabek Area. *The Winners*. 22 (1). pp. 1–14.

Kementerian Ketenagakerjaan. 2023. What is the Pre-employment Card Program.

Kredit Usaha Rakyat. 2016. Purpose and Objectives.

LPEM FEB Universitas Indonesia and UNDP. 2020. *Impact of COVID-19 Pandemic on MSMEs in Indonesia | UNDP in Indonesia.* University of Indonesia's Institute for Economic and Social Research and United Nations Development Program.

Measurable AI. 2023. *Asia Online Delivery 2019–2022: Food and Grocery.* https://measurable.ai/en-US/asia-food-delivery-report/.

Momentum Works. 2021. *Food Delivery Platforms in Southeast Asia: January 2021.* Singapore.

______. 2022. *Food Delivery Platforms in Southeast Asia: January 2022.* Singapore.

______. 2023. *Food Delivery Platforms in Southeast Asia: January 2023.* Singapore.

Morgan, P. and L. Trinh. 2021. Impacts of COVID-19 on Households in ASEAN Countries and Their Implications for Human Capital Development. *ADBI Working Paper* No. 1226. Tokyo: Asian Development Bank Institute.

Nielsen Singapore. 2019. *Understanding Indonesia's Online Food Delivery Market.*

OECD. 2020. Women at the Core of the Fight against COVID-19 Crisis. Paris: Organisation for Economic Co-operation and Development.

Olivia, S., J. Gibson, and R. Nasrudin. 2020. Indonesia in the Time of COVID-19. *Bulletin of Indonesian Economic Studies.* 56 (2). pp. 143–174.

Rajmohan, S. 2020. Helping our Helpers with GoModal. *Blog.* June 2.

Riddell, W. C. and X. Song. 2012. The Role of Education in Technology Use and Adoption: Evidence from the Canadian Workplace and Employee Survey. *IZA Discussion Paper.* No. 6377. Bonn: Institute of Labor Economics.

Shinozaki, S. and L. N. Rao. 2020. COVID-19 Impact on Micro, Small, and Medium-Sized Enterprises under the Lockdown: Evidence from a Rapid Survey in the Philippines. *ADBI Working Paper Series.* No. 1216. Tokyo: Asian Development Bank Institute.

SMERU Research Institute. 2020. Urgency of Improving Indonesia's Social Assistance System amid the COVID-19 Pandemic. *Insight.* July 27.

Sonobe, T., A. Takeda, S. Yoshida, and H. T. Truong. 2021. The Impacts of the COVID-19 Pandemic on Micro, Small, And Medium Enterprises in Asia and their Digitalization Responses. *ADBI Working Paper Series.* No. 1241. Tokyo: Asian Development Bank Institute.

Statistics Indonesia. 2020. *Census 2020.*

UN Women. 2020. *Leveraging Digitalization to Cope with COVID-19: An Indonesia Case Study on Women-Owned Micro and Small Businesses | UN Women Data Hub.* Jakarta: United Nations Entity for Gender Equality and the Empowerment of Women.

UNICEF. 2021. 85 Per Cent of Families in Indonesia Received Support on COVID-19 but More Efforts are Needed to Reach the Poorest—UN Report. *Press Release.* March 4. United Nations Children's Fund.